MW01165048

Shipwrecks of Newfoundland and Labrador

Shipwrecks of Newfoundland and Labrador

by
FRANK GALGAY
&
MICHAEL McCARTHY

Harry Cuff Publications Limited
St. John's, Newfoundland, Canada
1987

Acknowledgements

Appreciation is expressed to the *Canada Council* and the Newfoundland and Labrador Arts Council for publication assistance.

The publisher acknowledges the financial contribution of the Cultural Affairs Division of the Department of Culture, Recreation and Youth, Government of Newfoundland and Labrador, which has helped make this publication possible.

Cover design by Mr. George O'Brien. Photo Courtesy of The Illustrated London News.

First Printing, May 1987
Second Printing, January 1988

Printed in Canada by
CREATIVE PRINTERS & PUBLISHERS LIMITED
803-807 Water Street, St. John's, Newfoundland

ISBN 0-921191-15-4

DEDICATED

TO

CAPTAIN WILLIAM JACKMAN

Born at Renews, Newfoundland, May 20, 1837

Died February 25, 1877

AUTHORS' ACKNOWLEDGEMENTS

We would like to thank the following for their support and encouragement: Dr. Bobbie Robertson; Mr. David Davis, Mr. Anthony Murphy, Mr. Don Morris, Newfoundland Provincial Archives; Mr. Jack Martin, Memorial University Photographic Division; Mr. Thomas Myrick; Mr. Frank Graham; Mrs. Rosemary Galgay; Mrs. Queen Maloney; Mr. Elmer Harris; Mr. Bill Rowe; Mrs. Regina Mulcahy; Honorable Loyola Hearn, Minister of Education; Mr. William Hynes Jr.; Mr. Bill McDonald; Mr. Loyola Sullivan, National President of the Kinsmen Club of Canada; Mr. Gerard Healey; Mr. Jim Brazil; Mr. Damien Collier; Mrs. Carmel Power; Sr. Helen Corrigan; Rev. Gerald Benson, District Secretary, Newfoundland and Labrador Branch of the Canadian Bible Society; Mr. Lorne Wheeler; Mr. Bill Callahan; Mr. David Murphy; Mr. Keith O'Brien; Mr. Gus Galgay; Mrs. Anna McCarthy; Mr. Jack Fitzgerald; Mrs. Betty Curtis; Mrs. Nellie Conway and Mr. George O'Brien.

TABLE OF CONTENTS

Chapter

FOREWORD

SHIPWRECKS OF NEWFOUNDLAND AND LABRADOR is a book that tells the stories of some of the terrible sea disasters, that are so much a part and parcel of our history. It also records the heroic deeds of the brave Newfoundland men and women who in the face of almost insurmountable odds, risked their lives to save those facing certain death. It shows too, the compassion and sharing of a race of people who knew full well the dangers faced by those "who go down to the sea in ships."

Here are true stories of terrible disasters, of legends and stories that have been told and retold and long since become part of our folk history.

In an appendix are listed the names of some of those brave men and women who were claimed by the ocean. A second appendix provides a partial list of shipwrecks which took place near Newfoundland.

Written to appeal to a broad readership, this book should prove of great value in helping to preserve for future generations, a very valuable part of our Newfoundland culture.

Captain Michael D. McDonald

*Patrick Coombs of Portugal Cove South, Trepassey being lowered 200 feet by fishermen to retrieve bodies from the ill fated S.S. "George Washington" which was lost between January 18-23, 1877. (Photo: Courtesy of Mr. J. Martin, MUN Photo and Charles P. De Volpi's **Newfoundland** — A Pictorial Record)*

Chapter 1

NAVIGATIONAL HAZARDS, and The Early Recorded Wrecks In Newfoundland's Coastal Waters

The coastal waters of Newfoundland and Labrador have always held many dangers to shipping. There are more than seven thousand miles of coastline, hundreds of bays, coves, runs and islands, strewn with sunkers, sandbars and arctic ice. In addition mariners are prey to shifting ocean currents, high winds and fog. As a result the number of ships and sailors that have come to grief in Newfoundland waters is truly astronomical. Of all these dangers the two greatest threats to shipping in our coastal waters are ice and fog. In the days before lighthouses and fog alarms, the ice and fog took a high toll of ships and men.

Along the Southern Shore and South-West Coast it was the fog that posed the greatest danger. From 1894 to 1898 a study showed an average of 86 foggy days annually in that area from April to August at Cape Race. These dense fogs and the shifting ocean currents there gave the Cape Race area the unwanted title of "Graveyard of the Atlantic."

However, there are other areas of Newfoundland famous for their wrecks: Cape St. Francis, Cape Spear, Isle aux Morts, St. Pierre, Gull Island, Notre Dame Bay, and Baccalieu Island to mention but a few.

Combined with the 'everyday' dangers of uncharted waters, ice and fog, there were always the dangers posed by sudden storms. In 1775 for instance, one of the worst storms recorded to that date swept over the island with a huge loss of ships and lives. It was estimated that over three hundred people were drowned. In September 1876, a similar gale on the Labrador coast wrecked 25 fishing vessels. In 1882, another hurricane destroyed 22 vessels in Notre Dame Bay alone, and in 1885 there was again a great destruction of vessels on the Labrador. Then, in 1914, a March storm brought about two monumental tragedies: the loss of the *Southern Cross* and the *Newfoundland* disaster.

Against sudden gales and hurricanes there was no protection or safeguards, except to become well versed in weather signs and lore. These

1

'folk' methods of forecasting weather sometimes worked no better than today's satellites and computers.

In navigating in fog and ice the early captains and navigators often developed their own aids to navigation. In his book *"Voyage to Newfoundland,"* in 1818, Lieutenant Edward Chappell describes how the captain of an English warship approached the Newfoundland shores in fog.

On their arrival in Newfoundland waters, which the Captain knew from the distance travelled, the coast near St. John's was blanketed in fog, and for several days they could not fix their position because they could see neither the sun nor the stars. Knowing he must be near the Newfoundland coast, the captain alerted the various watches to listen for the sound of breakers.

Shortly after coming on watch one man with very keen hearing thought he could faintly hear the wash of waves on a shore. Although no one in the watch could hear anything, the captain took no chances. He ordered the anchor dropped, and waited for the fog to lift. When it did the man was proved right; they were only a short distance from land. Later during the same voyage the same man saved the ship again on the Labrador coast.

Of course not all captains were as insightful navigators as the captain of the *Rosamond,* and as a result there is hardly a cove, cape, or community in Newfoundland that has not seen at least one wreck in its history.

Yet there were ways to avoid going on shore, as a study of the Cape Race area showed following the shocking loss of life in the wreck of the *George Washington.* This study suggested a simple safety check when in the area. The report acknowledged the dangers of fogs and shifting currents, but stated that a ship coming towards Cape Race from the westward had only to sound the depth of water to know when it was close to land, for at a distance of ten miles from Cape Race and Cape Pine there is no more than thirty fathoms of water. Thus, if a ship maintained a depth of more than thirty fathoms in this area, it would never be in danger. Despite such good advice however, wrecks did continue in the Cape Race-Cape Pine area long after the report was published.

Up until the first quarter of the 19th century, we have few details of the many wrecks that occurred. Usually a reference is made without many details being given. From this time on, with the advent of a government system of lighthouses and fog alarms, much more detailed accounts are given of the sea disasters around our coast, both in official reports and in the local and foreign press.

From some of the early navigators and writers we do have accounts of a few of the early wrecks along our coast. Some of the wrecks before 1800 are as follows:

The very first ship to be lost on our shores could well be that of John Cabot, who is credited with the re-discovery of Newfoundland in 1497. Cabot made a second voyage to Newfoundland with six ships in the following year and did not return. Some believe that Cabot was wrecked off Baccalieu Island in Conception Bay, on the strength of a tradition that the name "John Cabot" was found carved into a cliff in Grates Cove, possibly an inscription carved by Cabot himself after the shipwreck. In support of this theory is a tradition which tells of a Beothuck who carried an Italian sword such as "Giovanni Cabota" or his crew might have worn.

A second ship of the early explorers to have disappeared in Newfoundland waters was that of Gaspar Corte-Real, the famous Portuguese navigator. Corte-Real dissappeared in 1501, while on his second voyage of exploration to Newfoundland waters.

The following year his brother Miguel came to Newfoundland in search of Gaspar, but he too failed to return.

In 1527, John Rut, an early English explorer, reported the loss of a ship called the *Sampson,* and another source in the same year mentions a ship being wrecked in the Straits of Belle Isle.

Captain Davis in 1587 visited St. George's Bay and reported the wreckage of two Basque whaling ships that had been driven ashore in a storm.

The earliest wreck found and identified in Newfoundland waters to date is that of the small British frigate, H.M.S. *Sapphire,* scuttled in Bay Bulls Harbour during the French attack of 1696 to prevent her from falling into the hands of the enemy. The wreck is now an under-water historic site, and one of the earliest identified wrecks in Canadian waters.

According to a local tradition at Conche, a French ship was sunk in the harbour in 1706. Her guns and decks were visable for many years on the bottom of the harbour.

In 1710, Governor Costabelle of Placentia made the first report of a wreck at Cape St. Mary's, an English privateer.

The British records for 1721 report two wrecks in St. Mary's. The first was the two hundred ton *Hecuba* under the command of Captain Loztal. She was lost on the rocks but there is no mention of any loss of life. A second ship *The Tezeza,* a vessel of 120 tons, also went ashore at St. Mary's with the loss of her skipper and two crew members.

The same year saw a wreck reported from Renews where a ship under the command of a Captain Davis, went ashore in a dense fog and was a total loss.

From Placentia in 1721, Governor Gledhill reported the fate of the *Betty,* a galley from London laden with winter supplies for the garrisons in Newfoundland: lost with all her cargo off Trepassey, on October 19th.

3

A ship bringing supplies to replace those lost in the sinking of the *Betty* also went ashore in St. Mary's Bay, but her cargo was saved and brought to Placentia.

The stories of many wrecks in the various coves and harbours of Newfoundland have been preserved only in folklore. One of these is the tale of the sinking of a pirate ship at Aquaforte, whose remains could be seen in the inner harbour until recent times. The pirates were being chased by a British man o'war when the captain sought to hide in Aquaforte. According to local tradition the ship went aground, so some of the crew blew her up with gunpowder and escaped with their ill gotten treasure.

At Shoal Bay near the Goulds, there is a similar story of a pirate ship being hard pressed then blown up to prevent her capture by the British authorities. The treasure from this ship is supposed to be buried at Shoal Bay and guarded by the ghosts of some of the pirate crew, who were murdered by their greedy captain. If there are ghosts at Shoal Bay they may be from the H.M.S. *Tweed,* a British naval ship which was wrecked there in 1813.

Newfoundland also has its share of unsolved mysteries of the sea, for there were many ships that left their home ports and were never heard of again. Among these were two vessels sailing out of King's Cove, Bonavista Bay. The *John* cleared from King's Cove for the seal hunt with a local crew in the spring of 1830 and never returned. The second ship was the *King* which sailed for Brazil with a load of dried cod and the only tidings were rumors she had been captured by pirates and all her crew murdered. There are numerous other examples from virtually every harbour on the island.

— The disappearance of the passenger steamer S.S. *Lion* has never been solved. She is thought to have blown up in Baccalieu Tickle in 1882.

— In 1847, the brigantine *Native Lass* was last seen going out the St. John's Narrows.

— The brig *Begonia* left Twillingate in December 1904 with six men and one woman on board; it was never heard of again.

— In 1919, the schooner *Haskel* from Bonavista left Griquet in early November and simply vanished from the ocean.

— In 1909, the schooner *Little Jap* left Deer Island, Bonavista Bay, for St. John's with thirteen people on board and disappeared without a trace.

— The *Rose,* a schooner belonging to Carbonear under the command of Captain James Kennedy, left Assiz Harbour, Labrador on October 15, 1877 en route to her home port. She carried thirty-seven people who never made port.

The sketch shows the sinking of John Cabot's ship "The Matthew" near Grates Cove, Newfoundland in 1498. (Photo: Courtesy of the Newfoundland Provincial Archives)

— In 1883 the schooner *Six Brothers* left Lower Island Cove for Trinity Bay in early May with fourteen crew and passengers, and was never heard from again.

On January 20, 1877, another large ship came to grief in Bristow Cove, about seven miles from Cape Race. There were no survivors and the ship was identified as the *George Washington* from some blankets that washed ashore with the ship's name on them. The ship was smashed to atoms and even recovering the dead bodies was very difficult. The tragedy was discovered when some fishermen saw a few dead bodies floating in the surf off Bristow Cove. They could not recover the corpses until a local man named Patrick Coombs was lowered on a rope from the cliffs above. Coombs succeeded in plucking 14 bodies from the boiling surf. Later other battered remains were taken from the ocean and buried with dignity on the cliffs above the scene of the tragedy. An inquiry was held on the loss of the ship, but as there were no survivors or witnesses to the wreck, there was nothing to indicate why the tragedy had occurred. The *New York Herald* felt that it was the lack of lighthouses and fog alarms along the coast that caused the tragedy. Like many other Newfoundland sea disasters, the facts will most likely never be known.

In the marine history of Newfoundland, there are many strange stories of wrecks and rescues, of great sacrifice and of terrible deeds, of heroism and avarice. Our history is filled with stories of tragedies of the ocean, and of the fearless men who "go down to the sea," just as their fathers and their grandfathers did before them. These stories and the heroes and heroines of today and yesterday are forever a part of us and of our Newfoundland culture, for we cannot hope to appreciate our ancestor's way of life if we do not take into account the constant danger of the sea.

Chapter 2

TRAGEDY AT MARINE COVE, ST. SHOTT'S
The Wreck of H.M.S. *Harpooner* November 10, 1816

On the 10th of November, 1816, the British transport ship *Harpooner* struck on the outermost rock of St. Shotts, and a great sea tragedy followed. The *Harpooner* had set sail from the port of Quebec City, on October 27th and was bound for Deptford, England. She was under the command of Captain Joseph Briant. The ship had been chartered by the British Government to bring back to England soldiers and their dependents of the Fourth Royal Veteran Battalion. The passengers numbered three hundred eighty men, women and children. Only a tiny number of their company survived the ordeal at Marine Cove, St. Shott's on that stormy November day.

The journey down the St. Lawrence River was pleasant and uneventful, but when they reached the Gulf of St. Lawrence the weather became stormy and heavy fogs made navigation difficult. In fact the fog was so thick that the Captain could not see land nor fix his position by the sun. Thus on the evening of November 10th they were unaware that the ship was headed dead for the cliffs of Marine Cove.

At a few minutes after nine p.m. the mate on watch felt the ship strike and called a warning that the ship was aground. This was not true, however, for the force of the winds and tides carried the ship free from the rock she had struck, but a few minutes later she struck again, heeled over, and began to fill with water. In the meantime the heavy seas continued to dash the ship against the rocks, and wash over her decks. Under this terrible buffeting it was clear that the ship would soon break up. In an attempt to lessen the strain, Captain Briant ordered the masts to be cut away. In doing this, several persons became entangled in the wreckage and were swept overboard. They were the first casualties of the wreck.

Then the pounding and force of the waves carried away the berths and stanchions between the decks, and a number of people were drowned or killed by being crushed against the loose baggage and floating casks, which now rolled free. The flooding between decks brought everyone to the top deck, and terror and confusion reigned, the frightened passengers expecting each moment to be their last. Under these circumstances the commands of the Captain and the officers of the battalion went unheeded. A number of people were crushed or pushed overboard as the crowd scrambled starboard side to get as high as possible out of the water.

Although there is no official record of such an attempt, a tradition among the people of St. Shotts says that a number of marines attempted to make it to shore. They were supposedly successful in landing in a kind of underwater cave. However, when they called out to those still on the *Harpooner* to tell them of their success, an avalanche of rocks buried the cave where they had found shelter. A second tradition says that two lifeboats were launched filled with women and children, under the command of one of the ship's officers, and attempted to pull away from the wreck in the direction of St. Mary's. However, a few minutes after their successful launching, the lantern in the lead boat was suddenly extinguished. By eleven p.m. most of the remaining lifeboats were washed away.

The stern lifeboat was still intact, and at five a.m. the first mate accompanied by four seamen set out in a last desperate attempt to try and make it to shore. The going was rough, but they made it. However, they could not return to the ship for it had been torn apart on the rocks in the inward passage. The men who had made it climbed a high rock and shouted out for the log line to be thrown up to them. The darkness and the heavy seas made this impossible, and the line fell short.

The survivors on the *Harpooner* had been buoyed up by the successful landing of the mate's party, but as the attempts to get a line ashore failed, despair again settled over them.

In a last desperate attempt to get a line ashore Captain Briant tied the log line to the ship's dog, and threw him overboard. With the log line tied around his middle and with the hopes of everyone on the Harpooner riding on him, the dog set out for the shore. Describing this awful scene later, one of the survivors wrote that, "no one but the people trapped on the doomed vessel could understand their feelings as the dog rose and fell with the huge waves."

The dog made it, and the mate and his men slowly hauled ashore the rope that was attached to the log line. Then after they were successful in securing the rope to the rocks the tricky business of bringing the people from the *Harpooner* to the rock began. The people had to hold to the rope and be pulled ashore, with the waves breaking over them all the way. A number of people from the ship were rescued this way. Some were insensible when pulled to the safety of the rock. There was one loss of life when Lieutenant Wilson lost his hold on the rope. He swam for a

This picture of an illustration of a boat heading home was typical of the tranquility of the HMS "Harpooner" on its voyage down the St. Lawrence before it was wrecked on November 10, 1816 in Marine Cove, St. Shotts, Newfoundland. (Photo: Courtesy of Mr. J. Martin, MUN Photo and the **Illustrated London** *News of December 17, 1881)*

9

few minutes, but was hit by a piece of wreckage and disappeared beneath the waves.

All through the morning of November 11th people were helped ashore by means of the rope, and by mid-morning 30 people had made the perilous journey. Then a new disaster struck. The rope broke from scraping on the sharp rocks. There was no way of getting another rope ashore, and so no avenue of escape was left to the more than two hundred souls left on board.

As the people on the rock watched, the waves grew higher and, breaking over the ship, carried many overboard. Then as families huddled together, the ship broke in two from stem to stern and all on board joined their companions in a watery grave, along with a large amount of gold carried by passengers.

The rock on which the survivors had landed was cut off from the mainland at high tide, so some of the last survivors had to remain there until dawn the next day to make it ashore. They had no food or shelter, but they did manage to kindle a fire from some of the wreckage of the *Harpooner*. The next morning they were got down from the rock by means of a rope ladder and made their way to the small house of the one fisherman then living in St. Shotts, which was about one and a half miles from the wreck.

The poor fisherman did not have supplies for such a large number, so a party of men set out for Trepassey about fifteen miles away. On their arrival at Trepassey they were immediately given food and shelter, and the magistrate, priest and merchants found places for everyone. A party of men from Trepassey went to St. Shotts for the remainder of the survivors, and brought back the weak and injured on their backs. Three persons remained with the fisherman at St. Shotts. One was the wife of a sergeant who had been delivered of a baby on the rock where they had landed. The other two were a woman who had suffered many bruises and a private with a broken leg. They remained at St. Shotts until well enough to travel.

After the other survivors had rested for a few days at Trepassey, boats were provided to take them to St. John's. In St. John's Governor Pickmore treated them well, and chartered the brig *Mercury* to take them home to England.

The survivors praised the actions of Captain Joseph Briant and the mate Mr. Atkinson, by whose efforts thirty-five souls were rescued. Perhaps the story of the *Harpooner* does not end here. A hundred years later a small fishing schooner was anchored in Marine Cove for the night. Only one man was on watch at about eleven o'clock when he noticed a light coming towards him. As it neared, he could see that the light came

The passengers of the HMS "Harpooner" included women and children. This dramatic picture of the loss of the Steamship "Clan MacDuff" in the Irish sea was typical of the horror experienced by the passengers of the "Harpooner." (Photo: Courtesy of Mr. J. Martin, MUN Photo and the Illustrated London News of November 5, 1881)

from an old fashioned lantern hung in the stem of the skiff. The lead boat was towing a second smaller skiff filled with women and children. Standing at the tiller of the lead boat was a big man with square jaws, wearing an old-fashioned blue coat. As the boats passed under the bows of the fishing boat, the man in the blue coat hailed the sailor on watch. "What is the course to get around Cape English?" The sailor told him and the two boats slowly rowed away into the darkness. The sailor was a bit uneasy and called the captain and other crew members up to have a look. They got on deck in time to see the light on the skiff melt into the darkness. After discussing the matter they came to the conclusion that another wreck must have taken place in the area.

In the morning they searched in vain, and then put into St. Shotts where the people told them that what they had seen was not the survivors of a new wreck, but rather the ghosts of the crew and passengers of the ill-fated transport ship *Harpooner*.

Chapter 3

RESCUE AT ISLE aux MORTS
The wreck of the *Despatch* July 12, 1828

Over the years there have been many wrecks with terrible loss of life in the Isle aux Morts area, in fact it is from these wrecks the community got its name: "Island of the Dead". Most of the wrecks are simply question marks in some dusty shipping records, the fate of their passengers and crews forever unknown to the loved ones they had left behind. However, because of the bravery of a Newfoundland fishermen and his family, one wreck in this area received international recognition.

It was the morning of July 12th, 1828, and in his cottage in the tiny community of Seal Cove, Isle aux Morts, George Harvey woke to the sounds of a raging gale. A fisherman, Harvey knew well the perils of the ocean, and especially the dangerous reefs and shoals around his home waters. Over the years he had witnessed many wrecks along the coast, and like his neighbours had helped to bury the corpses that floated up on the beaches or were caught in the kelp and rocks at low tide.

Through the night the wind increased in strength. By morning it had begun to subside, but now the ocean was in full fury, with thirty foot waves dashing against the shore and sending showers of spray to the tops of even the highest cliffs. Unable to sleep, George Harvey rose early, breakfasted on boiled fish, pulled on his out-door gear and went outside. He checked his wharf and stage, but in the protection of the cove they had successfully weathered the storm. His boat pulled up on a slipway well above high water mark was in no danger from the sea, although even in the sheltered cove there was a heavy sea running. Assured that all was well, he was on his way back home when he heard the sound of a gun, and saw a series of distress rockets go up in the sky.

Quickly Harvey climbed a hill behind his house. On reaching the lookout, he saw that another terrible sea tragedy was in the making.

About three miles up the coast from Seal Cove a large brig had struck an off-shore rock, and was in the process of being pounded to pieces by the mountainous waves. Her life-boats had been smashed, and the crew and passengers had no means of getting ashore from the doomed ship. In the forecastle, the only part of the vessel out of reach of the waves, huddled her 180 passengers and crew, awaiting their seemingly inescapable doom and sending up distress signals in the faint hope that someone could come to their assistance.

George Harvey's first thought was how to get a rope to the people trapped on the ship, though he knew that he could never buck the wind and waves single-handed. He quickly returned to his cottage and told his seventeen-year-old daughter, Anne, and her twelve-year-old brother Tom of the sight he had just witnessed. They immediately volunteered to assist in a rescue attempt. It was all George Harvey needed, and in a few minutes, he and his two children were launching their boat. As was his custom, their water dog 'Hairy Man' had already jumped aboard the punt, and taken up his position as forward look-out. Inside the relatively, calm waters of Seal Cove it was easy going, with George Harvey pulling away on one pair of oars and Anne and her brother on the other. Then they were out-side the shelter of the headland, and facing the full fury of an Atlantic storm.

Bending to the oars the three Harveys forced the little craft until they could more easily see the doomed ship's company, and read the name *Despatch* written on her bow. But the very fierceness of the sea made it impossible to go alongside and rescue the stranded people. It was also evident that if help was not soon forthcoming all the people on the ship would find a watery grave.

Then Anne Harvey suggested that they try sending the dog to the ship. It was a long chance, but the dog had braved the waves often enough before to fetch sea birds shot by his master. He was a tireless swimmer and obeyed every order his master gave him. Calling the dog from his perch in the stem of the boat, Harvey pointed to the people on the ship and ordered the dog to swim to them. Without hesitation the faithful animal jumped over the side and struck out for the *Despatch*.

The first wave caught the animal and buried him in its crest. Anxious-ly the people on the wreck and the Harveys waited for him to rise. The seconds ticked by and then he rose above the crest still swimming strong-ly, with only the top of his head above the waves. Time and time again the mountainous waves buried the struggling animal, but undaunted, he kept his way and at last reached the ship. Here willing hands quickly pull-ed him on board.

The dog was allowed to rest for only a few moments, for the ship was starting to go to pieces. Then with a light strong line tied about his mid-dle, he was again put overboard and ordered to go to the Harvey's boat,

14

Anne Harvey played a prominent role in assisting her father in rescuing the passengers of the Despatch which was wrecked at Isle aux Morts on July 12, 1818. This picture taken of a painting "Her First Hand at the Oar" by M. Renouf which was exhibited in the Paris Salon is reminiscent of the early days Anne Harvey enjoyed rowing with her father. (Photo: Courtesy of Mr. J. Martin, MUN Photo and the Illustrated London News of October 22, 1881)

which was with difficulty managing to keep head on to the wind. As the dog swam the line was carefully let out behind him.

Once again the drama of Newfoundland water dog against the elements was played out, with the lives of 180 people hanging in the balance. Sometimes the cresting of a wave buried the dog for several minutes and hope faded, but then he would surface again, his web paws pushing him closer and closer to the boat. Then he was alongside and was quickly lifted aboard. The Harveys wasted no time in getting to shore, and quickly landed the cable which was now attached to the line that the dog had brought. This cable was made fast to shore and the crew of the *Despatch* fashioned a breeches-buoy. Over this hard-won road to safety passed one hundred and eighty grateful souls, snatched from the angry maw of the sea by the unselfish heroism of one brave Newfoundland family.

For two weeks the Harveys had to share their meagre store of flour and other store-bought staples with their unexpected guests. Then George Harvey took some of the survivors to Port aux Basques to summon a ship, which took the greater part of them on to Quebec. The remainder were taken to St. John's by a British warship.

With the removal of the *Despatch's* survivors, life at Seal Cove returned to normal. But in Quebec and St. John's and at last even London, the story of the heroic rescue was told, and eventually reached the ears of King George IV, who was so taken by the tales that he had a special gold medal struck for presentation to George Harvey and his family. The inscription on the medal told the story of their daring rescue. As well, the stockholders of the marine insurance company Lloyds of London sent one hundred pounds stirling as a token of their appreciation.

Two years were to pass before the Harveys received their reward. Then on September 29th, the feast of St. Michael, the famous Anglican missionary, Archdeacon Edward Wix, presented the medal and the one hundred pounds to the Harveys, following a church service in their home. Accompanying the medal was a personal letter from the king congratulating them on a brave deed. Anne Harvey accepted the medal on behalf of her family.

Ten years later, on September 14th, 1838, the Harveys rescued twenty-five crew members of the *Rankin,* a Glasgow ship wrecked in the same area. Again Anne Harvey helped man the rescue boat. Despite a measure of international fame, Anne Harvey continued to live at Isle aux Morts. She later married Charles Gillam, and like the ending of the old fairy tales, lived happily ever after.

Chapter 4

CLAM COVE DISASTER
The Wreck of the S.S. *Anglo-Saxon,* April 27, 1863

The Southern Shore of Newfoundland is known for its thick fog at the best of times, and April 27th, 1863 was no exception. On this date the S.S. *Anglo-Saxon,* under the command of Captain Burgess, plowed through the heavy Atlantic swell to keep an unexpected date with death.

It was a bitter cold day for April, and howling winds swept over coast and ocean, keeping the passengers and most of her crew of the *Anglo-Saxon* below deck.

On her fatal last voyage the S.S. *Anglo-Saxon* carried a crew of 86 together with 48 cabin passengers and 312 emigrants from Great Britain and Ireland, off to seek new homes in the far Canadian West. These emigrants had paid eight guineas for their passage, and had had to provide their own bedding, cooking and eating utensils, and food. Needless to say the steerage was not the most desirable part of the ship. She also carried mixed cargo of cloth and iron goods and the Canadian mail. The *Anglo-Saxon* had been built in 1860, and was the flag-ship of the famous Allan Line. She was a fully rigged, three-masted vessel, equipped with both steam and sails. She was of 1,713 ton burden and was built of iron.

As the S.S. *Anglo Saxon* approached Cape Race that April morning she was using both steam and sail, as she usually did when on the Grand Banks and anticipating ice.

As she steamed along under full canvas, the *Anglo-Saxon* must have looked eerily majestic in the dim, grey world of fog and flying spray. Then at exactly 11:10 a.m. the ship's lookout cried out that there were breakers ahead on the starboard quarter. Even as the bridge telegraphed "full speed astern", the twin rocks and the cliffs of Clam Cove loomed in the grey fog.

William McMaster, the chief engineer, did his best. The great engines of the *Anglo-Saxon* went full speed reverse, but the ship's momentum was too great and, with a sickening crash, she struck heavily in the aft section. The engine room telegraph then rang "stop", and a moment later "full speed ahead", and Alec MacRae, the Second Engineer, was ordered to stand by the pumps and have every man do his duty. It was all to no avail, for the water poured into the forward stokehold and put out the fire and silenced the engines. There was now no hope to save the stricken ship.

At this moment Chief Engineer McMaster took the only safety measures he could. He eased the safety valve on the boiler to avoid immediate explosion and, as the engine room was rapidly filling with water, told his men to "keep their heads and save themselves." Not everybody kept their heads, however, as four hundred sixty-six people crowded the top deck asking what had happened. As they took stock of their situation, it was apparent that the force of the impact had lodged the *Anglo Saxon* between the Twin Rocks. As the waves pounded her against the rocks the gale force winds and the under-tow began forcing her slowly broadside to the low cliffs of Clam Cove.

Seeing the danger of being dashed against the Clam Cove Cliffs, the Captain immediately ordered that the bow anchors be put out to hold the ship securely between the Twin Rocks. Despite a panic among the passengers, the Captain and crew stuck to their duty. In the first three minutes after the ship had struck, three crew men jumped ashore from the bow-spit. Catching lines thrown to them from the ship, they worked frantically to secure a number of cables from the *Anglo-Saxon* to near-by rocks, hoping to hold the ship to the shore and steady her. As soon as the cables were secured, an improvised travelling basket was rigged, and immediately the work of getting the passengers ashore began. Eighty-three persons, mostly women and children, were in this way snatched from the churning waters that were quickly tearing the Anglo-Saxon apart.

Led by Dr. Alfred Patton, the ship's surgeon, and several other crew members who had been landed to care for the frightened women and children, the first survivors found the shelter of some woods at the top of the cliffs. Some of the men went back to the shore to collect driftwood for a fire, and to search for any food and clothing that might have come ashore.

Later some of this group walked four miles by the Imperial telegraph path to the Cape Race Lighthouse where the first information was sent to St. John's of the disaster. Immediately on hearing of the wreck, Captain John Murphy and his crew of the Associated Press Newsboat set out for Clam Cove. They brought food, ropes and axes and upon arrival helped to make fires and feed the hungry survivors still at the scene of the wreck.

Meanwhile, Captain Burgess attempted to launch the six life boats of the *Anglo-Saxon*. It is a sad reflection on the safety regulations of the time that even had it been possible to load all six lifeboats, they could

This picture shows the banks of Clam Cove Brook in the clearing where the fishermen buried one hundred of the recovered bodies of the passengers of the S.S. "Anglo-Saxon" which sank on April 27, 1863. (Photo: Courtesy of Mr. Thomas Myrick, former resident of Cape Race)

19

only have accommodated one hundred ninety-two persons, out of a total ship's company of four hundred sixty-two.

Under Captain Burgess's direction Lifeboat number one was positioned forward starboard. Lifeboat three was placed mid starboard, and lifeboat five at the aft starboard. Lifeboats two, four and six lay on the side towards the sea, where there was less problem from the high winds, but the waves were apt to smash the boats against the ship's hull. As the Captain and crew fought valiantly to launch the boats, the remaining passengers huddled together in terror. Number three lifeboat was launched with thirty-two souls, but was immediately stove in and sank with its occupants, mostly women and children.

As the *Anglo-Saxon* settled deeper and deeper, giant swells began sweeping her decks, carrying masts, gear, deck-house and other debris into the ocean. Those who could climbed into the rigging, but this too was soon swept away into the North Atlantic, carrying a large number of the crew to a watery grave. In fifteen minutes all the lifeboats had been launched, and the basket landings had come to an end.

Battered and pounded on the rocks the deck structure of the *Anglo-Saxon* began to disintegrate with topmasts and rigging falling on the deck. Then the stern began to sink lower and lower in the water, the decks broke open. Just sixty minutes after striking on the Twin Rocks, the *Anglo-Saxon* slipped beneath the waves. Through all the terror and horror of that hour, Captain Burgess was true to the tradition of the sea, and stayed with his ship to the end.

At the final moment when the *Anglo-Saxon* slipped under the waves, Captain Burgess and Third Officer Robert Allen were both thrown into the icy waters. Burgess swam for a few minutes but was then carried under and drowned. Third Officer Allen managed to swim to a part of the ship's saloon that was floating in the surf, and was later saved. The Chief Officer, John Hoare, jumped as the deck sank under him. He was picked up by one of the life-boats, which had stayed as close as they could to the ship in the hope of picking up more survivors. The survivors in this lifeboat were later picked up by the *Dauntless* and the *Cape Ballard*.

Following the end of the *Anglo-Saxon,* the lifeboats pulled away to try and find a place to land. Two boats made it to Cape Race, where they landed and joined those who had already come overland. The survivors in the other boats were later picked up by the rescue ships sent to the area.

The full details of the tragedy reached St. John's about nine p.m., and by ten-thirty, James Johnson Grieve of Baine Johnston and Company (the Newfoundland Agents for the Allan Line) had the firm's new sealing steamer, *Bloodhound* and the tug *Dauntless* on their way to the scene of the wreck. The *Bloodhound,* under the command of Captain Alexander

Graham, went directly to Cape Race to pick up the one hundred thirteen survivors who had taken refuge there. Eighty-four of these had been rescued at Clam Cove and walked overland, twenty-nine others had made it by lifeboat. The *Dauntless,* under the command of Captain Whitten, went to search for survivors in the Clam Cove area. She picked up ten persons the following day, who had been drifting on pieces of wreckage. A third rescue ship, the *Cape Ballard,* picked up eighty-four more persons from the drifting life boats.

In all two hundred and nine survived the wreck of the Anglo-Saxon, the other two hundred thirty-seven finding watery graves. Of the number lost fourteen were crew members, including the Captain, fifteen were saloon or first class passengers, and two hundred and eight were passengers of the steerage class. Of those drowned, the fishermen of the area recovered one hundred bodies. These were treated with dignity and respect, and buried in graves dug on the banks of Clam Cove Brook. Each grave was marked with a stone at the head and foot.

One of the survivors, the Reverend Charles Pemberton Eaton of Sketchworth Vicarage, who had been picked up in a lifeboat by the *Cape Ballard,* insisted on going back to Clam Cove to help identify the bodies and to assist in their burial services.

On May 2nd, 1863, most of the crew and passengers who had survived the ordeal embarked on board the S.S. *Bloodhound* for Quebec. The few remaining passengers left on May 5, 1863 aboard the mail steamer *Merlin* for Halifax. Two orphaned children remained in Newfoundland: Edward Walton aged three, and his sister Harriet Walton aged five. They were placed in the Old Church of England Orphanage, and remained there until September 8, 1871. The records of the Orphanage state as follows:

> The children [Edward and Harriet Walton] were brought to the orphanage by Mr. W. H. Mare. Later Dr. Crowdy sent their photographs to the Allan Line in Liverpool, and they traced the only living relative, a grandmother living in East London, who stated that their father had been a hairdresser/shoemaker, journeyman.

Edward went to work with Philip Hutchins, the Water Street Draper and later emigrated to the United States where he died. Bishop Feild took a great interest in Harriett, who later married, and became Mrs. Long. The noted motor-vessel, *Harriet Walton* was called after her.

There are many relics and artifacts in existence from the Anglo-Saxon such as silverware with her flag, a silver meat-dish, guns and other articles. In fact the Captain of the *Dauntless* reported that the second day after the tragedy, the waters around Clam Cove were filled with pieces of floating wreckage, including a large number of casks and boxes. The strangest relic, however, was a gold ring, found in the stomach of a cod fish by a St. John's fisherman in 1871, inscribed with the words "God Above Continue Our Love." The ring was eventually traced to a Mrs. Pauline Burnham, an Englishwoman who had gone down with the *Anglo-Saxon* and whose body had not been recovered. The fisherman was paid fifty pounds for the return of the ring to the deceased lady's relatives.

By 1900 the burial site at Clam Cove had become so badly eroded that something had to be done to restore the graves. The Government of the United States provided money to build a stone wall around the graves site, and to restore the graves. This was done, and today the cemetery can still be seen, a large green mound protected by the wall from further erosion. The remains of the *Anglo-Saxon* still lie somewhere in the fifteen fathoms of water near the "Twin Rocks" where she struck.

Chapter 5

LABRADOR RESCUE
Wreck of the *Sea Clipper,* October 9, 1867

One of the greatest acts of heroism recorded in the annals of marine history occurred off Spotted Islands, Labrador in the height of a raging storm of hurricane proportions on October 9, 1867. It was one of the worse storms recorded on the coast of Labrador, a shore known for furious gales. The drama unfolded as Captain William Jackman and a friend took a casual walk from the environs of the community to view the big sea crashing on the rugged shore. As they approached a headland Jackman spotted a vessel which had been driven onto a reef about six hundred feet from shore. The bottom of the ship was badly damaged by the sharp rocks and the raging seas were tearing her hull to pieces. Although only thirty years old Captain Jackman was an experienced seaman and quickly realized the ship could not hold out much longer. He also knew it would be impossible to launch a rescue boat and that the crew and passengers were in a nearly hopeless predicament. The *Sea Clipper* had a total of twenty-seven people on board that day. They included her captain and crew and the passengers from another vessel damaged by an earlier collision with the *Sea Clipper.*

Captain William Jackman wasted little time. He sent his companion back to the village of Spotted Islands for men and ropes, and then without hesitation pulled off his heavy boots and jacket and plunged into the icy waters. Undaunted by the mountainous waves he began an arduous swim towards the *Sea Clipper* and her 27 terrified passengers and crewmen who watched his progress, scarcely believing he could force his way through the boiling surf.

As a boy in the Southern Shore community of Renews, Jackman had often battled the full force of the Atlantic in summer play. As a young sailor and later sealing captain, he had come to know the bitter cold of northern waters and the dangers of the northern coast. However it was

23

not his bodily strength but some inner iron determination that gave him the strength to swim the six hundred feet to the *Sea Clipper.*

On boarding Jackman immediately took a man on his back and made the return trip to shore. Eleven more times he swam the raging gulf and eleven more persons from the wreck were brought safely to shore. He was about to enter the water for the twelfth time when his companion arrived with men and ropes to help in the rescue. Taking a rope, Captain Jackman tied it around his waist, and again plunged in. Fifteen more times he fought his way to the *Sea Clipper,* in all rescuing twenty-six people from certain death.

As he landed the twenty-sixth, Jackman asked if everyone was now ashore. The answer was in the negative. There was still one more, a lady who had been too ill to assemble on deck with the others and who they said must now surely be dead. Without hesitation Captain Jackman prepared to face the boiling surf again, despite the pleadings of the survivors and his friends who begged him not to risk his life further. Despite their assurances that the woman was dead, Jackman again swam the six-hundred foot maelstrom.

There was no sign of life on the water-logged wreck, which was now threatening to capsize. Undaunted, he climbed aboard and went aft to the cabin. There, too ill to move and with her head barely above water, he found the last terrified passenger of that ill-fated craft. Jackman took the fainting woman in his arms and carried her on deck. There he tied her body to his own, and for the last time plunged into the icy waves and again he battled his way to shore. Now, at last he could rest.

It was a Justice of the Peace for Labrador, Mr. Matthew H. Warren, who first brought the heroic deed of Captain William Jackman to public notice in a letter to Bishop Thomas Mullock, the Roman Catholic bishop of St. John's, dated November 1867:

> I deem it my duty to write you, who I trust, will make known to your flock and others the highly meritorious brave and humane conduct of Captain William Jackman, who during the violent hurricane of the 9th of October was the means of saving many lives in the imminent risk of his own . . .

It was through the efforts of Mullock and others in the Colony that Jackman's courageous deed was brought to the attention of the Royal Humane Society in Britain. A year later a despatch was received at Government House in St. John's, from the British Secretary of State, the Duke of Buckingham. The Despatch was dated September 14, 1868 and was as follows:

> I have been requested by the Secretary to the Royal Humane Society to transmit to you the accompanying Silver Medal and Scroll which had been awarded by the society to Captain Thomas Jackman [sic] for saving the lives

This picture of a distressed vessel in a storm was typical of the weather encountered by the "Sea Clipper" before she was wrecked off Spotted Islands, Labrador on October 9, 1867. (Photo: Courtesy of Mr. J. Martin, MUN Photo and the **Illustrated London News** *of November 12, 1881)*

of many wrecked persons at Spotted Islands, Labrador on 9 October, 1867. I request that you will cause the medal to be forwarded to Captain Jackman whose address is stated to be care of Mr. H. Warren, St. John's, Newfoundland and that you will report to me that you have done so.

On December 19, 1868, His Honour the Administrator of the Newfoundland Government presented Captain William Jackman with the Silver Medal of the Royal Humane Society, which he humbly and graciously accepted.

His wife, the former Miss Bridget Burbridge, and his immediate family were very proud of his heroic accomplishment. Jackman, however, made little of the honour accorded him by the International Society, it being simply part of the creed of the Jackman family of Renews that you had to strive for excellence and persevere until a task was completed. It is said that when the hero told his father of the rescue Captain Tom's only comment was, "If you had not brought that woman ashore, I'd have never forgiven you."

For nine years after this heroic deed Captain Jackman went about his usual tasks. He commanded ships and men, and faced again the dangers of the Labrador coast. Yet the ordeal of 1867 had sapped even his iron strength, and he slowly began to fade and on February 25, 1877 one of Newfoundland's greatest heroes died. He was mourned by his beloved wife and six children, his well-known brother Captain Arthur Jackman, his father Captain Tom, and all of Newfoundland.

One newspaper of the day wrote that a life had been cut short which was full of hope and promise, and that even at thirty-nine he had already realized an amount of usefulness and merit that is given to few men to achieve in such a brief span of years. On the day of his funeral all the businesses of St. John's closed and all the flags flew at half-mast, as the hero from Renews was laid to rest in Belvedere Cemetery.

Chapter 6

LETTERS FROM GULL ISLAND
The *Queen of Swansea* Tragedy, December 12, 1867

On the morning of December 6, 1867, the brigantine *Queen of Swansea* left the port of St. John's with passengers, general cargo and the Christmas mail for the Union Mine at Tilt Cove, Notre Dame Bay, Newfoundland.

The *Queen,* as she was known on the St. John's waterfront, was a vessel of three hundred fifty tons, that traded across the Atlantic from her home port of Swansea, Wales. The ship was under the command of Captain John Owens and carried beside the captain, a regular crew of seven Cornish seamen. On her December voyage to St. John's she carried two passengers from Swansea, a Miss Hoskins and her brother William, en route to Tilt Cove to spend Christmas with their parents. At St. John's the *Queen of Swansea* took on four other passengers, a lady and three gentlemen, all bound for Tilt Cove. One of the passengers was a Mr. Felix Dowsley, a St. John's apothecary, who was taking up the position of medical officer with the Union Mine. Although not a doctor, Mr. Dowsley was known locally as Dr. Dowsley because of his medical skills.

Due to his lack of knowledge of Newfoundland's northern waters, Captain Owens also took on board a local pilot, Mr. Patrick Duggan, to assist in navigating the local waters. Shortly after leaving St. John's harbour a violent storm arose, and it was feared that the *Queen of Swansea* had sunk with all hands on board. A week later the worst fears for the safety of the passengers and crew of the ship seemed to be confirmed, when the cover of Patrick Duggan's trunk and some other wreckage washed ashore at Twillingate. A search was made of the area but nothing further was found and the fate of the brigantine remained a mystery.

Then in April of 1868 there was further news of the ill-fated ship and a story of suffering and death was revealed that horrified and shocked the Newfoundland public. The full account of what had happened to the passengers and crew of the *Queen of Swansea* was revealed when Captain Mark Rowsell of Leading Tickles accidentally found the remains of some of the *Queen's* passengers and crew. Captain Mark was returning from a sealing trip when his vessel became becalmed near Gull Island, a steep granite rock a few miles off from Cape John. While they were waiting for a breeze, two of the sealers launched a boat to go bird hunting. In a small gulch in the island, they shot at and wounded a bird that flew to the top of the rock before dropping. Not wanting to lose their kill, and the seas being calm, they landed on the island and scrambled up in search of the bird. Then they saw ropes hanging from a rocky ledge about half way up the face of the cliff. They investigated and found what looked like the skeletons of two humans, the bones being piled together in a heap. A little further away on the same ledge of rock they found a piece of sail canvas frozen into a bank of ice. When they cut the sail away they found a number of frozen bodies. Immediately they went back to their ship and reported their grisly find to Captain Rowsell.

When Captain Rowsell examined the scene, he knew that he had found some of the missing passengers and crew of the *Queen of Swansea*. Leaving everything as it had been discovered, he sailed to Tilt Cove and told of his discovery, asking for volunteers to go back with him and his men to Gull Island to bring back the bodies. Patrick Mullowney, a brother-in-law of Duggan the pilot, and Mr. Gill who was a coroner, along with a number of other men accompanied Captain Rowsell back to the scene of the tragedy. They brought axes, crowbars and some rough coffins.

The men removed the bodies and the authorities at St. John's were advised of the discovery. Then, in the pockets of the dead, the men from Tilt Cove found notes that told vividly of the hunger, pain and desperation of those unfortunate victims of the sea. In the first note discovered, Captain Owens had written:

The *Queen of Swansea* got on the rock of Gull Island, Cape John, Newfoundland in lat. 49 deg. 59 min, and long. 55 deg. 11 min. W, or thereabouts, on 12th December, 1867. Consisting on board, altogether seven hands of the crew and the master, which was eight in number of the ship's company, and six passengers and a pilot — two of the passengers being female; altogether on board fifteen souls. The captain and mate and seven men and two females landed on the Gull Island by means of a rope at six o'clock A.M., on the 12th of December, 1867, just as we stood, neither bread nor eatables, nor clothes. Boatswain, pilot and one of the ship's crew went away with the ship, and a married man, [Power] who was one of the passengers. All these four perished with the ship. This is written on the island after landing, by me.

(Signed) JOHN OWENS
Master, *Queen of Swansea*

These unknown sailors experienced the same violent seas as the passengers of the "Queen of Swansea" which was lost December 12, 1867. (Photo: Courtesy of Mr. J. Martin, MUN Photo and the **Illustrated London News** *of Christmas, 1881).*

The second notebook was that of Felix Dowsley, and in a series of three letters to his wife he told in graphic details part of the suffering they endured until death released them from their agony. His first letter was dated December 17, five days after their being castaway on the island.

Gull Island, off Cape John,
Tuesday, Dec. 17, 1867.

My darling Margaret:-

As you are aware, we left St. John's on Tuesday morning, the 6th inst. On the evening of that day a dreadful gale came on, which lasted about two or three days. We were driven off about one hundred sixty miles to sea. I thought every moment the vessel would be upset or swamped; but it appears she was spared a little longer for a similar fate. We ran into a gulch on the Island on the morning of Tuesday, the 12 inst. about six o'clock, when the sea was raging and running mountains high. She only remained there ten or fifteen minutes, which was not sufficient time for all hands to save themselves. All were saved with the exception of two of the crew, Duggan the pilot, and Mullowney's stepbrother. We were dragged up the cliff by means of a rope tied round our waists. Not one of us saved a single thing but as we stood, not even a bit of bread; this is our fifth day, and we have not had a bit or sup, not even a drink of water, there being no such thing on the island. It is void of everything that would give us comfort. It is so barren and black that we cannot get wood to make a fire to warm us. Our bed is the cold rocks, with a piece of canvass, full of mud to cover us. You may fancy what my sufferings are and have been. You know I was never very strong or robust. My feet are all swollen, and I am getting very weak. I expect that if providence does not send a vessel along this way to-day or tomorrow, at the farthest, some of us will be no more, and I very much fear that I shall be the first victim; if so, you will not have the gratification of getting my body, as they will make use of it for food. I am famishing with the thirst. I would give the money I took with me, yes! all I ever saw for one drink of water. If I had plenty of water I know I should live much longer. I feel a dreadful feverish thirst, and no means of relieving it. Oh! is it not a hard case that I cannot get even a drink of water. Oh! did I ever think my life would end in this way, to be cast away on a barren rock in the middle of the ocean, and there to perish, with cold, hunger and thirst, and my bones to be bleached by the winter's frost and the summer's sun, and be food for the wild fowls! Oh! is it not sad to think of this, and such a little thing would save us! We are only eight miles from Shoe Cove, where we would be received with open arms. Now my darling Margaret, as I plainly see that in a few hours I must appear before my God, I wish to say a few words about your future prospects. [Here Mr. Dowsley gave some private and personal instructions to his wife and then concluded with a last request should his remains be found]. Embrace my darling children and tell them to be obliging and kind to each other, for without this they cannot hope to prosper. Tell them their unfortunate, unhappy father leaves them his blessing. Should our fate be known before the spring, if............................ would come around he would be able to get my body or bones, which I would like to have laid in Belvedere. If I had you, or at least, if I were with you and my dear children, and had the clergyman, I don't think I should fear death half so much. I must now, my darling, take my last farewell of you in this world. May we meet and enjoy one another where there is no sorrow, no trouble, no afflictions.

I leave you my love, my blessing.

Your loving but unfortunate husband
F. DOWSLEY

But Dr. Dowsley did not die so easily, and the following day he penned a second short letter to his wife.

Wednesday, Dec. 18, 1867

I have been out to see if there might be any chance of a rescue; but no such thing. I am almost mad with thirst, I would give all I ever saw for one drink of water, but I shall never get it. We are all wet and frozen. I am now going under the canvas to lie down and die. May God pity and have mercy on my soul!

But again Dr. Dowsley did not die, and on Christmas Eve, he penned a last sad letter to his wife and family in St. John's.

Gull Island, off Cape John, Dec. 24th.

My Darling Margaret: — We are still alive, and only that. We have had no relief ever since, nor any sign of it. We have not tasted a bit of food of any kind with the exception of dirty snow water that melts around under our feet, which we are very glad to devour. The place we are sheltered in, if I can call it a shelter is up to our ankles in water. Oh! what a sad Christmas Eve and Christmas Day it is for me! I think I can see you making the sweet bread and preparing everything comfortable for tomorrow. My feet were very painful last night. I was in complete agony with them. My clothes are completely saturated. Oh! I never knew how to appreciate the comforts of a home or a bed until now. If I were home, and to have you and the children beside me, and have the clergyman, I think the trial would be small compared to what it is now: but we shall never see one another again in this world. I had no idea we should have lasted so long. Our case is now hopeless; there is no hope for deliverance. My sufferings have been beyond description since I landed on this barren rock . . . Oh! how I dread — I would write more, but feel unable. Oh! my darling, if I could but once see you and the children I would be satisfied. Embrace them for me. [A few words of loving farewells to his family and a request for prayers follows, and he closed this last letter by signing himself].

Your living but unhappy husband
F. DOWSLEY

Then there was the third note by William Hoskins. Unfortunately this notebook was lost or misplaced shortly after its discovery, but according to some contemporary writers who do not give the note a date it simply

31

read: "We are starving and frozen and must draw lots so that some might keep alive longer should help come." There is another line added in a trembling hand. "We have drawn, the lot fell on my poor sister. I have offered to take her place. The horror of it all!"

There is no further mention of the terrible scene that must have followed, but William Hoskins' skeleton was one of the two heaps of bones found by the sealers, the other was that of one of the crew members. It is interesting that Dowsley is silent on the terrible decision taken by the group to kill one of their number to sustain the others, and later to choose a second victim for the same purpose. It is this terrible action that adds an extra touch of horror to a sad story of misery and hardship that ends in the death of everyone on the island.

The tragic story told by the notebooks of the victims of the Gull Island tragedy was published by the St. John's newspapers, and the tragic and horrifying circumstances surrounding the shipwreck of the *Queen of Swansea,* passed into the realm of folk legend.

On April 25th, the *Newfoundlander's* correspondent in Fortune Harbour wrote a letter to that paper telling of the northern efforts to find the missing ship, and the details leading up to its discovery. This report mentions the fact that lights were reported on the island but no one bothered to investigate, and that is the final chapter in the story of the wreck of the *Queen of Swansea*. According to a local tradition in the area, a simple boy who used to walk about the community of Shoe Cove after dark reported having seen lights on the Island; no one believed him. On Christmas Eve, he again told people of seeing the light, but no one listened or bothered to go and investigate.

In the report of the findings by the *Newfoundlander's* correspondent at Fortune Harbour, it was remarked how strange it was that when the search for any wreckage of the brigantine was on, no one had bothered to check out Gull Island. The story in the *Newfoundlander* ended with the statement that "It is a sad, sad, history which will not soon be forgotten." As he had requested, the body of Felix Dowsley was brought back to St. John's and his remains were buried in Belvedere Cemetery. Public pressure was brought on the government of the day to build a shelter on Gull Island and stock it with a little food so that another tragedy in the future might be averted. Some years later a monument was erected in memory of the people who had died in the tragedy of the sinking of the *Queen of Swansea*.

Chapter 7

THE ST. MARY'S TRAGEDY, March 1, 1875

On March first 1875, the magistrate of St. Mary's went to St. Vincent's (then known as Holyrood) to check on a report that a ship stuck in the ice about two miles off Cape English, was being abandoned by her crew. The magistrate arrived at St. Vincent's to find that a large number of local residents were gathering on the beach with the intention of boarding the vessel to secure her cargo. The mate and crew of the vessel, which they said was the *Violette,* had managed with a good deal of difficulty to cross the ice and make it to land, but the captain of the ship, according to the mate, was too ill to even attempt the journey over the ice. On hearing this, several men from St. Vincent's volunteered to go aboard the ship and bring the captain to safety. The men gathered on the beach were waiting for the captain to be brought ashore before boarding the abandoned vessel.

The magistrate, fearing there might be some trouble, sent for James Burke, the local police constable, to join him at St. Vincent's. Burke arrived just after mid-day in time to see the men from St. Vincent's bringing the captain to shore. He was so weak and ill the men had to take turns carrying him on their backs, but they managed to get him ashore.

Patrick Stamp, a resident of St. Vincent's, took the captain to his house and gave him every care and attention. The captain was so weak he couldn't even sit up but had to be carried to Stamp's house on a slide. By the time the captain had been brought ashore it was mid-afternoon, and all the weather signs were pointing to a storm. Despite this however, the men on the beach set out to board the *Violette.* According to Thomas Hines, one of the men who later gave evidence at a hearing into the chain of events that followed, they did not go in a single group, but in small parties of two or three men.

It was rough going over the ice to the large pan where the ship was frozen, but according to Hines' evidence they did succeed in getting aboard the vessel and, it would appear, in removing most of her cargo of salt, sugar, coffee and rum. However, when they attempted to get ashore again, they discovered that the wind had swung round to the east-north-east, and the ice had slacked off, leaving a large patch of open water between the men and the shore.

It was around this time that the threatening storm broke in all its fury, and there was nothing left for the men to do but try to get back aboard the *Violette*. This proved to be much more difficult than it had been the first time, for the wind had begun driving the ice-pan and the ship out to sea.

The men now tried to gather together in large groups, but in trying to get from some of the smaller pans three people fell into the icy waters and were drowned. At last they managed to gather together into two parties, each desperate to save themselves. They spent a cold and hungry night on the ice, but the next day seventeen of the men in one party managed to get back on board the *Violette*. The other party which was made up of ten men, drifted away on an ice pan. Some of those had fallen in the water in getting from the smaller pans to the larger pan, and were in desperate condition.

That first night they had sheltered behind a large ice boulder at one end of their pan. All night the bitter March wind tore at them, and the thermometer dipped well below the freezing point. Just before dawn Michael Vail and James Whelan died from the cold and exhaustion. A little later on the same day, Thomas Boland died. The seven survivors huddled together and prayed for rescue. Another day passed, and they were growing weaker: George Rowsell and his son, and Mike Vail's son died. Then the weather cleared and they could see Cape Pine in the distance.

The sight of land gave them renewed strength and somehow they managed to walk fifteen miles over the rough and treacherous ice and landed at Cape Pine.

In the meantime, the twenty-one men who had made it to the *Violette,* had been carried over one hundred miles out to sea, with the ship still frozen in her icy prison. Then the wind changed and they were brought back about forty miles from land.

The hull of the *Violette* was sound as were her sails and rigging, but she was almost totally empty of provisions, except for some rum, and flour. According to James Tobin, one of the survivors, the flour was put aboard the *Violette,* by a Mr. Michael Lundrigan of Peter's River, at great risk to his life when the ship was six miles from his house. Without this flour the men would have starved for they were more than ten days trapped in the seemingly doomed ship. At first the rum had been welcomed, but the wiser men of the party, observing that there was a feeling among some of their number that they might as well drown their sorrows, quietly let the rum run overboard.

In the meantime the news of their predicament had been flashed to the outside world, and it made the headlines in the major St. John's papers. At first they reported forty-two men trapped on the ice with twenty dead. Later thirty-four was the number given, which included those who had made it on board the *Violette.* On March fifth, a telegram to Sir Ambrose Shea from Salmonier listed nineteen men as missing on board the *Violette.* This telegram was published in the St. John's *Public Ledger.*

The government of the day promised immediate assistance to the wives and children of those lost in the disaster. As well the H.M.S. *Tiger* was despatched at once to search for any survivors.

On March ninth, a rumour circulated that the *Violette* had been sighted and reached by a boarding party. However, this rumour proved to be false, and on March sixteenth the *Public Ledger* reported that there was still no news of the missing men, including the fifteen supposed to be on the *Violette.* The paper also stated its opinion that all of those who had not managed to board the *Violette* were most likely lost. Following this the paper stated the next day that there were many fresh reports and rumours, but that nothing reliable would be known until a ship came upon the drifting *Violette,* whenever that would be.

Then it happened, the brig *Lady Mary* arrived in St. John's with eight of the survivors. These men had a story to tell. They said that twenty of them had made it to the *Violette,* the day after they left the beach at St. Vincent's, and had remained aboard her until rescued. During this time they had suffered much from cold and hunger. They were on the point of giving up hope, when on Thursday, March eleventh, a schooner, the *G.S. Fogg,* on a voyage from St. John's to the West Indies came upon the drifting *Violette.* The *Fogg,* after some difficulty, got close enough to take off the men who had been trapped aboard her for ten days.

On their arrival on board the *G.S. Fogg,* they were delighted to find the survivors of the other group, who had been picked up at Cape Pine on Saturday, March 6. Later the *Fogg* had put the rescued men aboard two other inbound vessels, the *Lady Mary,* and the *Trusty.*

The *Lady Mary* brought in the following men: Ed. Nowlan, R. Critch, Danny White, James Barry, Richard Connors, John Murray, Thomas Hines and John St. Croix.

The men placed on board the *Trusty* were: Michael Tobin, John Barry, Thomas Barry and James Murray. The *Trusty* had been in trouble when she came in contact with the *G.S. Fogg,* being short of both provisions and fuel. Captain Spense of the *Fogg* supplied the *Trusty* with food, and the hull and spars of the *Violette* provided them with fuel. She was bound for Harbour Grace but was unable to enter that port because of ice. She later made it to another Conception Bay port.

The remaining ten men on the *Fogg* were then transferred to the S.S. *Nuremberg,* which took them to Baltimore, U.S.A., where they arrived on March 29th. On April 29th the ten men were returned to St. John's by the S.S. *Newfoundland.* All the men's expenses were paid by Sir Hugh Allan.

The ten men who had travelled so far but returned safely were: Andrew Mooney, Thomas Mooney, William Reubin, Patrick Tobin, James Tobin, John Fewer, James Peddle, Thomas Dunn, Ben St. Croix, and fourteen year old James Grace.

Of the thirty-four men and boys who had set out to board the *Violette,* thirteen had either drowned or died from exposure. Those who died were: Michael Power, John Power, Michael Vail and his son, Patrick Dobbin, Michael Barry, Thomas Bowen and his son, George Rowsell and his son, Pat Layden, James Grace and James Phelan.

When the news of the disaster had first been made known, Mr. Collins, the M.H.A. for St. Mary's, opened a public subscription to assist the families of those who had died. On April 15th, 1875, he acknowledged receipt of 155 pounds 13 shillings for "The St. Mary's Relief Fund," which was then distributed to the widows and orphans of those who had died.

Shortly after the men had been rescued from the *Violette,* the mate and Captain of that ship claimed that they had been robbed of some of their personal effects while in St. Mary's. A court hearing was held into their complaint, but police constable Burke who had been present in St. Vincent's when they landed testified that they had not once complained of any losses during his stay at St. Vincent's, and that all their personal gear had been very carefully looked after by the people. The hearing decided that the mate's complaint had no basis and there was no further investigation.

The March disaster of 1875 was the worst single sea disaster to happen in that area, and the bizarre story of the *Violette* became one of the stock tales of cuddy and stage head for the residents of St. Mary's Bay as part of their heritage from the sea.

Chapter 8

THE *GREENLAND* DISASTER
March 21, 1898

No chronicle of Newfoundland's fatal relationships with the sea and weather would be complete without some mention of the terrible toll taken by sealing disasters. Since a "sealing disaster" entails a crew becoming separated from their ship, it cannot truly be called a "ship wreck". However, the causes and the tragic results are frighteningly similar.

The *Greenland* was built in Aberdeen, Scotland in 1872, for the Montreal Steam and Fishing Company. The ship measured 151 ft. in length and was 27 ft. wide and 16 ft. deep. In 1881, the *Greenland* changed owners when she was purchased by the Newfoundland firm of John Munn and Company, for the purpose of prosecuting the seal hunt and engaging in the Newfoundland fish trade.

On three occasions the *Greenland* was the first sealing steamer to arrive back in port. On April 4th, 1875, she was first arrival with 26,383 seals and, under very tragic circumstances, she was first again in 1898 with only 1,300 seals.

Despite her bumper trips in the seventies, the *Greenland* seemed to have had more than her share of bad luck, especially after her purchase by the Munn Company. It was whispered along the waterfront, that like the more famous *Great Eastern,* she carried a curse. Her first encounter with bad luck came on September 9th 1884, just two years after her purchase by Munn's. On that day, while being prepared for a trip to Labrador, she caught fire and sank in her moorings in St. John's Harbour. However, although badly damaged, she was refloated and repaired and everything went well with the ship until the spring of 1898. It was a beautiful, sunny morning as hundreds of people lined the old wooden wharfs of the St. John's waterfront to wish the sealers "a bumper trip" and "bloody decks," as the fleet prepared to face the ice floes in what was then one of the most important parts of the Newfoundland economy.

The S.S. *Greenland,* under the command of Captain George Barbour, carried a full complement of 207 men under the Baine Johnston Co. flag. She steamed out the Narrows in company with the *Neptune, Walrus, Iceland, Aurora, Leopard* and *Diane* amid the blowing of whistles, the ringing of bells and with flags and bunting steaming in the wind to encourage those men who would risk their lives on the frozen ice-floes. Outside the Narrows, the Greenland headed north in search of the main patch. She reached the Funk Islands on March 12th and struck the seals 70 miles north by northeast of the Funks.

It was too late on the evening of Saturday, March 12th for the *Greenland's* men to go over the side, and sealers did not hunt on Sundays. So, it was Monday, March 14th before the crew of the *Greenland,* in company with the men of the *Diana, Iceland,* and *Aurora,* began panning seals. To Captain Barbour and his men it was a good beginning for what could possibly become a "bumper load."

Meanwhile back in St. John's there was no news from the sealers at the Funks. These ships did not carry wireless and so there was no direct means of communication with the shore. The first news of the sealers was a copy of a bulletin posted in the window of the St. John's Telegraph Office on March 26th. The whole community read with fear and anxiety of the terrible tragedy that had befallen the crew of the S.S. *Greenland.*

The telegram was datelined March 26th, 1898, from the fishing community of Bay-de-Verde, to W.B. Grieve of Baine Johnston and Company, from Captain Barbour of the *Greenland.* In very terse terms it outlined the terrible tragedy that had necessitated cutting short the *Greenland's* voyage and immediate return to port. The telegram read:

S.S. *Greenland* arrived Bay-d-Verde. Too heavy to run, Sad misfortune—LOST FORTY-EIGHT MEN in heavy gale; more badly frost bitten and will need hospital care. Twenty-five dead bodies on board; remainder could not be found. Advise where to go.

Mr. Grieve wired Captain Barbour immediately with the following reply:

My heartful sympathy for you and the poor men. Come on here where arrangements are being made for living and dead. Do you apprehend disaster to any other ship?

Captain Barbour answered in the negative. It was only the *Greenland* that had been involved in the tragedy.

After the bulletin had been posted in the telegraph office, throngs of people gathered around the Anglo-American Telegraph headquarters anxiously waiting for additional news of those involved in the tragedy. Many of those gathered around the telegraph office were relatives and friends of the men who had gone to the ice on the *Greenland.* Since there was

This picture of the sealing fleet led by the "Arctic" breaking through the ice of St. John's Harbor was typical of the conditions encountered by the S.S. "Greenland" before its departure to the seal hunt. (Photo: Courtesy of Mr. J. Martin, MUN Photo. Sketch drawn by Schell and Hogan from a sketch by J. W. Hayward for "Harper's Weekly," April 5, 1884)

39

no further news after the initial bulletin, and no particulars of the disaster in the original telegram, the anxious people after a while slowly wended their way to their homes filled with anxiety and uncertainty as to the fate of their friends and loved ones. There was nothing they could do but wait for the arrival of the *Greenland* and hope for the best.

The following morning the S.S. *Greenland,* with flags at half-mast, entered the harbour and steamed slowly to its berth at Baine Johnston's wharf. Then from Captain Barbour himself the waiting people heard details of the terrible disaster that had overtaken the *Greenland's* crew.

Up until March 21st everything had gone very well. They were "in the fat", and it looked as if they would make an excellent voyage. On that Monday morning, which dawned dull and cloudy with a brisk northern wind, Captain Barbour put his four watches on the ice. The First Watch was put out in a south-easterly direction from the open lead of water in which the S.S. *Greenland* lay. Then the ship steamed northeast, approximately three and a half miles through the open lead until the ice was reached. There the other three watches were sent out by Captain Barbour. This done, the *Greenland* steamed back to where the First Watch had been put out. All hands were busy killing and panning seals until six o'clock that evening.

In early evening the weather suddenly changed without warning. A strong wind blew up from the north, accompanied by heavy drifting snow. Immediately on the commencement of the storm the First Watch was taken on board. Captain Barbour's first priority was to pick up the other three watches before darkness set in.

However, the bitterly strong winds began to wedge the ice tightly together, and in a matter of minutes the open water disappeared and the pack ice moved in on the *Greenland*. Despite the best efforts of the captain and crew the *Greenland* could not make any headway in the heavy ice. Certainly she could not go to the assistance of the three watches who had been landed three and a half miles to the northwest. With each passing minute the storm grew in intensity. All that night Captain Barbour did the only thing he could, he kept the *Greenland's* whistle going in the faint hope it might help guide the missing men to safety.

At the onset of the storm the men on the ice had stopped panning seals and gathered together to await Captain Barbour and the *Greenland*. It was only after they had decided to walk back to the ship that they discovered that they were stranded on the ice. A three mile lake of water had opened up between them and the *Greenland,* making it impossible for them to reach the ship on foot.

The stranded sealers took what measures they could to survive. Ropes and gaffs were used to make fires to roast seal carcasses, and the men tried in every way to keep going. George Tuff of Newtown, Bonavista Bay said: "We only kept ourselves alive by stamping, jumping and beating our hands, kicking one another, for if we sat down at all we would never rise again . . ."

Six men died from cold and exhaustion before dawn, and with the coming of day, the storm seemed to increase in intensity. Then, when there was still no sign of the *Greenland,* the men broke up into smaller groups of two and three men intent on saving their own lives. Several groups set out in different directions to find the *Greenland.* Blinded by the snow and half-crazed with cold, exhaustion and hunger, some of the men walked out into the open water and were lost. All day Tuesday they wandered aimlessly about, knowing instinctively that walking was their only hope of keeping alive; that to sit and rest meant death. Then around four o'clock in the evening the wind began to die down, the snow stopped, and over the ice came the faint sound of the *Greenland's* steam whistle.

The desperate survivors of the storm heard it, and a sudden surge of hope gave them the strength to hold on for just a little while longer. The stronger ones began to stumble and crawl towards the sound of the steam whistle. They were observed from the *Greenland* and two boats were instantly launched to go to the rescue of those unfortunate sealers.

All through the night the boats searched the open leads of water looking for the men who had wandered off. When daylight came the whole crew of the *Greenland* were sent out to search.

Captain Barbour got word to the *Diana* and *Iceland,* and they too helped in the search and rescue operation. The combined efforts resulted in the rescue of many men from the ice, but some of them were very badly frostbitten. When the search was called off forty-eight men were dead or missing and presumed dead. Twenty-five bodies were recovered and placed aboard the *Greenland* which now headed for home.

Fate, however, decreed that the *Greenland* should not have an easy trip. The wind came up and reached gale force with accompanying snow, and the *Greenland* had to seek shelter in Bay-de-Verde. It was from the telegraph office in this community that Captain Barbour sent the first news of the disaster to the owners of the *Greenland.*

Now, it seemed that the bad luck whispered about on the docks was really following the unlucky *Greenland,* for while she lay at Bay-de-Verde waiting out the storm, her mooring chain broke and she struck bottom near the shore. The crew immediately set to work to shift coal in order to alter her weight and she refloated on the tide without any loss of life. The bad luck continued for when the storm died down and when the *Greenland* set out for St. John's she came close to hitting the Biscay Rock off Cape St. Francis. Finally, the look-out mistook the entrance to Quidi

Vidi for the Narrows and again the *Greenland* nearly wound up on the rocks.

As the ship came up the harbour and the whole population of St. John's seemed to converge on Baine Johnston and Sons premises the police had to be stationed at the entrance to the wharves to keep back the crowds. Only a few of the *Greenland's* crew, their faces and hands bound up as a result of frostbite, were on deck. Then began the sad task of unloading the bodies of the twenty-five dead sealers. They were brought to the Seamen's Home, to be laid out and prepared for burial.

On Tuesday, the first coffin was brought out to the view of thousands of the sad and tearful citizens of St. John's. Then, the remains of the respective sealers were conveyed to their home communities, where the individual funeral services were held.

One of the papers of the day stated that the following verse rang out from many a city church choir on Sunday, March 27th, 1898 to mark the sad occasion.

Eternal Father, strong to save,
Whose arm doth bind the restless wave
Who bidd'st the mighty ocean deep
Its own appointed limits keep.
O hear us when we cry to thee
For those in peril on the sea.

Immediately following the *Greenland* disaster, a public subscription fund was set up by the leading citizens and politicians to help the wives and children of those who had died. The fund was officially known as the "*Greenland* Sufferers Relief Fund." It closed on July 26, 1898 after $17,000 had been subscribed.

News of the *Greenland* disaster had also been telegraphed to England, and on March 28, 1898 a dispatch was received from the Right Honorable the Secretary of State for the Colonies, to his Excellency the Governor of Newfoundland.

"Her Majesty has heard with much regret *Greenland* disaster and commands me to express sympathy with wives and families of sufferers. Wish to express my own sympathy.

Chamberlain"

The dead sealers were buried, the money collected through public subscription was distributed among the survivors and the sad memories slowly faded. The *Greenland* continued in operation and went to the ice each spring, until 1907, when her luck ran out, but this time without loss of life. Once again a sudden violent storm came up, and as in the great storm of 1898, the *Greenland* was squeezed by the rafting ice. It smashed her stauntions and bulwarks, and she began to take on water. As it became

42

apparent that the ship was slowly sinking, her crew left her walking over the ice to the other sealing steamers nearby. The last 25 men were taken off the *Greenland* by the S.S. *Bloodhound* just before she went under.

The ill-luck that had dodged the *Greenland* had at last finished her. Still, as long as stories of the sea are told, the S.S. *Greenland* will be remembered, for the tragedy of 1898 has passed into the realms of Newfoundland folk history.

This picture is of a model of the S.S. "Southern Cross" which disappeared on March 31, 1914 on its return to St. John's from the annual seal hunt. (Photo: Courtesy of the Newfoundland Provincial Archives)

Chapter 9

AN UNSOLVED MYSTERY OF THE SEA
The Disappearance of the S.S. *Southern Cross*, March 31, 1914

In the spring of 1914 two great disasters struck the Newfoundland sealing fleet, both caused by the same terrible storm of March 31st. The first disaster is well documented, as there were many survivors to tell the tale of the horror that hit the crew of the S.S. *Newfoundland* on that mad March night. The second disaster, the disappearance of the S.S. *Southern Cross* with one hundred and seventy-three men, while an even greater tragedy, is still a mystery, for there were no survivors to tell what happened and to this date not even any wreckage from the ship has ever been positively identified.

As the survivors of the *Newfoundland* disaster arrived in St. John's before the disappearance of the S.S. *Southern Cross* was known, they took up most of the headlines, and for several weeks after her expected arrival, people were still hopeful that the *Southern Cross* would turn up safely. As a result the second disaster never had the same impact as the *Newfoundland* Disaster, but the ultimate fate of the *Southern Cross* is still a puzzle that many seamen have tried to explain, and where and when she sank is still unknown.

The S.S. *Southern Cross* was built in 1886 in Arendal, Norway, and first served as a Norwegian whaler under the name *Pollux*. The ship was owned by O. B. Sorensen and was engaged in the Norwegian whale hunt for eleven years. The Lloyd's Registry of 1914 described the *Southern Cross* as a sailing ship 146 feet, 5 inches long, 39 feet, 7 inches wide with a deck to keel depth of 17 feet, 6 inches. In 1898, the *Pollux* was bought by Carstens Borchgrevink, a seasoned Antarctic explorer, to be used on an expedition to the Antarctic. He had two new engines installed and changed the ship's name to the *Southern Cross* after a constellation of stars in the southern skies.

The S.S. *Southern Cross* became famous in London, England when Borchgrevink was successful in having members of the British Royal

Geographical Society sponsor him and his crew on an expedition to the Antarctic. The *Southern Cross* sailed on her first Antarctic expedition from Hobart, Tasmania on December 19, 1898. She made two trips to the Antarctic in order to drop off and pick up explorers. In 1899, the *Southern Cross* made marine history when she went through the Great Ice barrier and entered for the first time the unexplored Ross Sea. There was great jubilation in London when the news of Borchgrevink's achievement was made known, he and his men having at that time come the closest to the South Pole.

After her success in the Antarctic, the *Southern Cross* was sold to Daniel Murray and Thomas Crawford of Glasgow, Scotland, who sent her on her first voyage to the Newfoundland seal hunt in 1901, under the command of Captain Darius Blandford, a veteran sealing skipper.

On her first trip to the ice, the *Southern Cross* was a great success. She was the first ship to arrive back in port with a full load of pelts, a "bumper trip," in the sealers' language. On that first voyage the *Southern Cross* brought back 26,563 seal pelts. For the next fourteen years the *Southern Cross* went to the ice each spring. She made some bad voyages and some good voyages, but never did she break her record of 1901.

In the spring of 1914 the *Southern Cross* was again prepared to go to the ice. On this voyage her master was Captain George Clarke of Brigus. George Clarke had the reputation of being a good sealer, but he lacked experience as an ocean-going captain. He was a tall man in his mid forties who had a good sense of humour and got along well with his men. George Clarke was also a man ambitious for wealth, fame and honour. There was fierce competition among the sealing captains to win the coveted silk flag awarded each year to the first sealing captain to make it to port with a "bumper load," and George Clarke dreamed of the day when he would win that silk flag and have a big pay-out for himself and his crew.

There was some difficulty in getting experienced sealers that spring of 1914, and when she sailed on the twelfth of March, the majority of the crew were under 25 and very inexperienced in sealing. Reports on the actual number of crew and sealers vary somewhat, but it would appear that the *Southern Cross* sailed from St. John's with a regular crew of ten and one hundred sixty-three young, eager sealers. This voyage of the old sealer was not to be to the Front, but to the Gulf of St. Lawrence and although she lagged behind the other sealers soon after leaving port she made it to the Gulf, and despite heavy ice conditions made a good voyage.

The exact number of seals secured by the ship's crew on this voyage is not known, but estimates based on the way the ship lay in the water vary from 17,000 to 25,000 pelts. All those who saw the *Southern Cross*

46

on her return voyage from the Gulf agreed that she was very heavily laden and lay deep in the water.

As the *Southern Cross* did not carry a wireless set, there was no direct news from her after she left St. John's. However, a report from Channel at 6.30 p.m. March 29th, 1914, said that the *Southern Cross* had passed Channel with all flags flying, obviously racing for St. John's and the coveted silk flag. There was no further report of the ship until the morning of March 31st, when at eleven a.m. she was sighted by Captain Thomas J. Connors of the coastal steamer *Portia* about five miles west south west of Cape Pine.

That morning a terrible storm had come up suddenly and Captain Connors was making for port. The *Southern Cross* had appeared suddenly out of the storm-swept ocean, so close to the *Portia* that she passed only a cable length behind her. Captain Connors described her as being very low in the water, all flags flying and smoke belching from her smokestack as Captain Clarke drove her at full speed through the gathering storm. The high winds and heavy drifting snow had reduced visibility to nearly zero, and the *Southern Cross* could be seen only dimly before she disappeared again into the blinding snowstorm. The *Portia* blew her whistle and the *Southern Cross* answered before she disappeared from sight. Captain Connors had no doubt that Captain Clarke was making for shelter in St. Mary's Bay to ride out the storm. That brief encounter with the *Portia* was the last time the *Southern Cross* was ever seen.

Following Captain Connors' reported sighting, there was great excitement among the friends and relatives of the *Southern Cross* sealers as to whether she would be the first in port and win that greatest sealers honour, the silk flag.

But first in port came the survivors and the bodies of those who died in the *Newfoundland* disaster and in the great surge of public sympathy and pity for the widows and orphans of the *Newfoundland's* crew, the *Southern Cross* was momentarily forgotten. It was felt that an older vessel like the *Southern Cross* would take longer to make it to St. John's after the storm, so her arrival was awaited at any minute. After some days passed and there was still no sign of the ship, the government sent the S.S. *Kyle* to search for wreckage, later joined by the *Fiona* and *Seneca*. No wreckage was found.

There are only two reported sightings of any kind of wreckage that might have come from the *Southern Cross*. The first was by the Captain of another sealer, the S.S. *Bloodhound* who reported seeing a large mass of floating debris about ninety miles south-east of Cape Broyle. The weather, however, was so rough at the time that the *Bloodhound* could not get close enough to make any kind of positive identification, but it was speculated that it was wreckage from the ill-fated *Southern Cross*. The second report circulated around the St. John's waterfront in the summer of 1914 that some actual wreckage from the missing ship had been picked up on the coast of Ireland. The story was that planks from the prow of a ship bearing the partial inscription . . . . THERN C . . . and a broken lifebelt with the *Southern Cross* written on it had drifted ashore. There was never any official confirmation of this, so it is likely that it was just another rumour making the rounds of St. John's wharves and ale houses.

At first, when the *Southern Cross* did not come into port when expected, men recalled another occasion when she had been forced to go offshore to weather a storm; and expected that she would turn up in a week or so. When she did not turn up, it was suggested she had sunk out in mid-ocean, and this explained the absence of wreckage or of bodies. Others felt she had gone down somewhere off Cape Race, with her hatches nailed shut and the helmsmen lashed to the wheel, although there was obviously no way of knowing such details. Other seamen discussed the sea-worthiness of the missing sealer. Some people argued she was a fine strong steam-sealer, especially designed to operate in heavy ice, and they pointed to her success in reaching the Ross sea in 1899. Their opponents agreed the *Southern Cross* had been a fine strong ship, but now they felt she was just a rotten old galley that should have been retired from such dangerous work as sealing. There was general agreement that the *Southern Cross* was high bulwarked for a wooden ship, which made her difficult to manoeuver in really heavy weather. The sealing captains in general believed that it would have been difficult to bring the fully-loaded *Southern Cross* about in a storm, and this would limit the defensive measures a skipper could take if he found himself in real trouble. One other factor was very important: as the *Southern Cross* had been built as a sailing ship and had her engines installed some years later, it had been necessary to place the engines as low on the keel as possible to keep her stabilized. If she started taking water her engines would swamp quickly, leaving her at the mercy of the waves.

The general opinion among the seafaring men of Newfoundland was that Captain Clarke had decided to make a run for St. John's in order to be the first ship in that he misjudged the intensity of the storm, and by the time he realized the full danger could do nothing but keep her headed into the wind and try to make it around Cape Race. When it is decided to ride out a storm, an experienced captain would have taken certain steps. The deck cargo would have been tightly secured and the hatches battened down. Then the helmsman, very likely the captain himself, would have been lashed to the wheel with the rest of the crew going below. This was

The Southern Cross docked in St. John's (Photo: Courtesy of Newfoundland Provincial Archives and Mr. Bren Kenney)

a common-enough procedure in desperate times and if the ship was sturdy enough she would survive.

It could be speculated, then, that the high bulwarks of the *Southern Cross*, her heavy load of seal pelts, and her low mounted engine all contributed to put her beneath the waves. It is easy to imagine that as the storm grew in intensity, tons of water would be trapped in the high bulwarks. (Captain Connors in his report on his sighting of the *Southern Cross* reported that "her decks were running green," and that she seemed half under water.) The trapped water would soon have begun to seep through the hatches. In a ship with high mounted engines this would not have been too important: in the case of the *Southern Cross* it was a potential disaster, for in a very short while the accumulated water could put out her fires, leaving the ship wallowing helplessly in the grip of the giant waves.

To add further educated speculation about the fate of the *Southern Cross*, imagine her engines dead, beginning to settle, rising more and more sluggishly, with no power to keep her head on to the wind. As the heavy seal pelts became more and more saturated, the ship would lose her buoyancy and sink slowly beneath the waves. With her hatches battened down, the crew below decks and the helmsman lashed to the wheel, she would corkscrew to the bottom of the ocean. There would be neither bodies nor wreckage to mark the spot where she sank.

The *Southern Cross* did not return from the ice fields, that we know. From the chance encounter of Captain Connors we know the ship was in the St. Mary's Bay area on March thirty-first, loaded and running at full speed through a gathering storm. That is all we can say for sure, and a Sealing Commission appointed to look into her disappearance could only find that her loss was "An Act of God."

Chapter 10

A FORTUNE BAY TRAGEDY
The Sinking of the *Marion,* June 18, 1915

Newfoundland has many strange tales of the sea, but few are stranger than the story of the ill-fated banking schooner, the *Marion.* Like many tales of the sea, the *Marion's* story touches on the supernatural. The evidence is scarcely enough to satisfy a historian: the tale rings truest when told on a dark night, when the sea rages.

The *Marion* was a seven dory banking schooner owned and operated by the Burkes of St. Jacques. On June 10th, 1915, the *Marion* left Burke's Cove under the command of Captain Ike Jones, a noted "fish-killer", never known to back away from a fight regardless of the odds. Besides Captain Jones, the ship carried a crew of 16 men, who came from several different communities in Fortune Bay.

On his way to the fishing grounds Captain Jones had to pass by the French island of St. Pierre and, as was often the custom, he decided to put in there to pick up a few needed supplies and to have a last fling before settling down to the business of getting a load of fish. When Captain Jones announced the stop-over, there was a little concern expressed by some of the crew, for on the incoming voyage, they had stopped there and been involved in a great row with the crew of a French beam trawler. Still, they knew better than to oppose their captain once he had made a decision.

The port of St. Pierre at this time was crowded with French, American and Newfoundland ships. Whether by accident or design, Captain Jones found himself next to the French trawler whose crew had been involved in the fight on the trip in. To add insult to injury, the *Marion* in docking scraped along the steel side of the beam trawler. This brought insults and jeers from the watching French crew, which were answered in kind by the captain and crew of the *Marion.* Later when they had spruced themselves up, Captain Jones and his crew went up to one of the cafés. After the night wore on a bit they came in contact with their old enemies from the trawler. The result was a great free-for-all, which did nothing

51

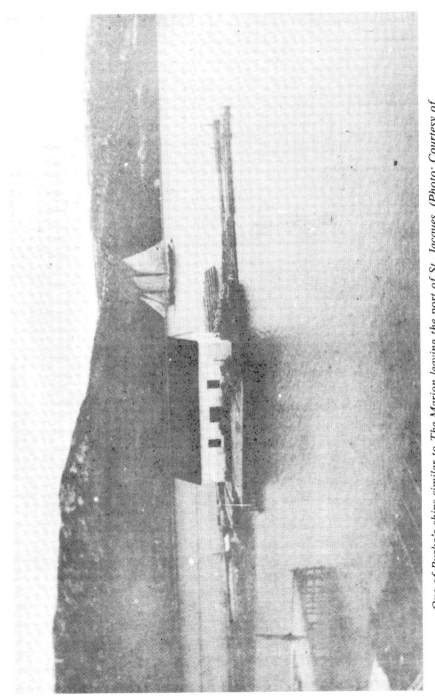

One of Burke's ships similar to The Marion leaving the port of St. Jacques. (Photo: Courtesy of Mr. Maurice Burke)

to improve matters between the two parties, especially as Ike Jones had "pounded out" the trawler's captain, who was an Italian.

Boasting of their victory the proud Newfoundlanders walked back to their ship, taunting the French crew in their defeat.

The next morning, as they hoisted their sails in preparation for leaving, Captain Jones made a final gesture of defiance — firing a musket across the bow of the trawler. Then the wind filled the *Marion's* sails and she moved off down the harbour. But as she sailed away, the workers on the dock, who heard the angry words of the beam trawler's skipper, shook their heads and muttered that the *Marion* would never be seen again. About an hour after the *Marion's* departure, the beam trawler got up steam and also left the harbour. The trawler returned before nightfall, but the *Marion* was never seen again.

The following morning at St. Jacques' the mother of the *Marion's* cook was looking out her kitchen window when she saw her son rowing towards her from Burke's Cove. As she watched him row the dory toward their wharf, she thought to herself that either the captain or one of the crew of the *Marion* must be ill, for them to return home so quickly. She watched her son row into the wharf, tie on the dory and go into the stage. She put on the kettle and set about preparing a "mug-up" for him. The kettle boiled and she made tea, but there was still no sign of him. She went to the door of the kitchen, opened it and called out to her son. There was no answer from the stage.

She waited a few more minutes, then throwing a shawl over her shoulders, she went down the rocky path to the stage. She listened, there was nothing but silence. She called his name. There was no answer, so she pushed open the stage door and went in. It was empty. She quickly ran out on the wharf. It too was empty and there was no dory tied there. Then she knew it was her son's token she had seen.

She went back to her house expecting the worst, and told her family and the neighbours of what she had seen. They comforted her, but they too knew the meaning of a token. The days passed but there was no news. The days grew into weeks and still no tidings of the *Marion* or her crew.

As the weeks grew into months the story of the fight between the beam trawler's crew and the *Marion's* crew was whispered about, and people shook their heads in disbelief. After a reasonable time the crew were given up for dead and the *Marion's* disappearance became just one more mystery of the sea.

The years passed and over their grog old timers would shake their heads whenever there was mention of the *Marion*. Perhaps someone would whisper the old story of the suspected foul play on the part of the beam trawler. Then word came to Fortune Bay that a dying sea captain either

The home port of the "Marion" was Burke's Cove, St. Jacques, Fortune Bay. Circa 1915. (Photo: Courtesy of Mr. M. Burke)

in Paris or St. Pierre, had confessed to sinking the ill-fated *Marion* and murdering her crew.

The old captain's story was that, enraged at being beaten up by Ike Jones and his crew, the men of the beam trawler had vowed vengeance. They had left port shortly after the *Marion* and some miles out on the St. Pierre Banks, armed with guns and knives, they had boarded the *Marion* and slaughtered her captain and crew. One of the last crew members of the *Marion* to survive was the young cook from St. Jacques. In a vain attempt to save himself he climbed to the top of the mast. However, he was trapped in the cross-tree and had his throat cut by the angry trawler's crew. His body was then flung into the sea. Having paid their grudge the trawler crew scuttled the *Marion*.

So ended the mystery of what happened to Burke's *Marion,* but still on foggy nights when the ocean glows and there is the rumble of surf on the rocks, some have claimed that they saw the *Marion* sailing onward to her date with an ill-starred destiny.

This picture shows the HMS "Raleigh" entering St. John's Harbor around 1920. She was lost in Forteau Bay on August 8, 1922. (Photo: Courtesy of the Newfoundland Provincial Archives)

Chapter 11

THE LOSS OF H.M.S. *RALEIGH*, FORTEAU BAY, August 8, 1922

The H.M.S. *Raleigh* was built just after World War One, and launched in 1919. In 1922, she was commissioned as part of the British North Atlantic Squadron. In the summer of that year she was sent on a cruise of Newfoundland waters. The *Raleigh* was classed as a light cruiser of twelve thousand tons. She measured 605 feet in length, and was capable of a maximum speed of thirty knots. On her summer cruise she carried a full complement of over seven hundred officers and men.

The *Raleigh* paid a visit to Corner Brook and in the second week of August set out for the coast of Labrador. On August 8th, she was on her way from Port Saunders to Forteau Bay. The ship encountered thick fog and heavy seas as she steamed north through the Strait of Belle Isle. As it was the first cruise for the ship in the area, neither the captain nor his officers were experienced in the dangers of icebergs while navigating in northern waters. They were proceeding towards their destination at full cruising speed when the men on the forward deck suddenly signalled a bridge of ice directly ahead.

The helmsman responded and frantically turned the ship hard to starboard to avoid collision. The manoeuvre was successful and the *Raleigh* narrowly missed collision with a giant iceberg, which was at the entrance to Forteau Bay. The manoeuvre saved the ship from running into the giant iceberg, but unfortunately it put the large cruiser in the very dangerous position of having to navigate the narrow entrance to Forteau Bay in very shallow waters near a rocky shore. As they entered Forteau Bay the fog grew even thicker, and so enshrouded the *Raleigh* that the crew could not literally see one foot in front of them. Speed was reduced to 6 knots, and like an ancient ghost ship, the H.M.S. *Raleigh* kept her course and crept on through the thick blanket of fog towards her destination.

Then suddenly and without any warning from the lookout, the H.M.S. *Raleigh* struck. There was a heavy grinding sound, and the rocks of Forteau

Bay ripped a 360 foot gash through the belly of the proud ship of war. The speed and size of the *Raleigh* carried her on over the rocks, and she went further aground between L'Anse Amour and Point Amour, finally settling offshore near Point L'Amour lighthouse about 200 yards from the shore. The Captain of the *Raleigh,* realizing that it was impossible to get his ship free due to the high winds and heavy seas in the area, called for volunteers to take a lifeline ashore in a cutter.

A number of men and non-commissioned officers under the command of a young commissioned officer answered the call and a cutter was immediately launched. They pulled away from the ship and headed towards shore. The seas were very high and the sudden gusts of wind made it difficult to keep the cutter steady. An extremely high wave struck the cutter and she went over, throwing the men into the water.

One of the young naval officers in the cutter grabbed the lifeline they were carrying, and holding it in his teeth struck out for the shore. He made it to land and secured the line. Then the same young hero, seeing that one of the other crew members of the cutter was in difficulty, dove back into the turbulent seas and rescued a man who had been knocked unconscious by being thrown against the rocks. As a result of this accident eleven of the volunteers were drowned, but the lifeline was in place, and the rest of the officers and crew were evacuated from the ship in liferafts tied to the lifeline, by which means all got safely to shore.

The H.M.S. *Raleigh* had struck on the rocks about 4 p.m. and it was 7 o'clock in the evening before all the crew had landed. The survivors had only what they stood in, for the rest of their belongings had been lost with the ship. Finding food and shelter for the crew became the first task of the ship's officers. The lighthouse at Point L'Amour, about a quarter of a mile away from the site of the wreck, became their first shelter. About 600 men spent the first night there, sleeping wherever they could find a place to lie down from the tower to the out-buildings.

A party of officers travelled the five miles overland to Forteau and asked the people to assist in putting up some of the stranded men. The community, including the local Grenfell nursing station, responded well. All available space that could hold a bed or a bunk was utilized, and the people of the area prepared to do what they could to assist the survivors.

At the Nursing Station twenty-five beds were prepared for sailors and fifteen for officers. The staff of the station stayed up all night waiting for the men to arrive. However as it was very dark and rainy the men spent that night in the three houses at L'Anse Amour and the lighthouse at Point Amour. The next day, Admiral Sir William Pakenham of H.M.S. *Calcutta,* which had arrived at the scene of the wreck, informed the Grenfell Mission Station that he was expecting a ship to arrive to take the sailors back to England. However, this plan fell through and so 400 survivors were brought to Forteau to await transportation home. The arrival of the four hundred men in Forteau, which had a normal population of 177, strained the resources of the whole community, including the Mission station, which fed the officers. The sailors lived on their own rations.

The personnel of the Nursing Station were very busy attending to the needs of the survivors, many of whom had bad cuts and bruises on their feet from walking on the rocks without boots. The other houses in Forteau took in the rest of the survivors and did the best they could. The Orange Hall was set up as a mess hall for the sailors to cook their meals.

The sailors from H.M.S. *Calcutta* showed their appreciation for the welcome their fellow sailors had received, by providing band concerts to the great enjoyment of the local people. A special band concert was held on August 11th in which men from both the *Raleigh* and the *Calcutta* took part. Captain Bromley of the *Raleigh* was in very low spirits following the loss of his ship, so on August 12th twenty-two officers from the two ships held a sing-song in the reception room of the Grenfell station, with Captain Bromley as their guest. The sing-along was a great success and lasted over three hours.

At long last the CPR passenger ship S.S. *Montrose* arrived at Forteau, and took most of the *Raleigh's* crew back to their home port. The 200 remaining survivors of the wreck were picked up on August 27th, and Forteau was able to get back to normal.

The Captain and crew of the *Raleigh* were loud in their praise of the kindness and helpfulness of the people of Point Amour, L'Anse Amour and Forteau. As a token of their appreciation before leaving, Admiral Pakenham donated fifteen tons of coal to the Nursing Station. The gift was welcomed by the people, for coal was a difficult commodity to get on the Labrador coast. As well the Admiral gave them a framed picture of the H.M.S. *Raleigh,* with a silver plate and an inscription.

Two days after the *Raleigh* struck the rocks her fate was decided. A wrecking tug, the *Royal Strathcona* had come from Quebec to assess her damages, and after divers had gone down and examined her bottom, the *Raleigh* was declared a total loss. During their wait for transportation from Forteau, the *Raleigh's* crew removed what they could from the wreck. After the crew's departure, the *Raleigh* was declared open for salvage, and the local residents salvaged a lot of lead and copper from the wreck. Her large propellers were salvaged by a Corner Brook firm using explosives and a large floating crane. Some Newfoundland schooners involved in the Labrador fishery also got some materials from the wreck. One of her lifeboats was later used as a herring skiff at St. Jacques, Fortune Bay.

In 1926, there were further attempts at salvage, and a Halifax-based ship took seven of the *Raleigh's* powerful 15 foot guns as well as the sighting mechanism. The removal of these guns caused some questions in the British press about such weapons falling into the hand of private individuals. As a result the British Admiralty dispatched an explosives team to blow up the *Raleigh*. They succeeded and most of the *Raleigh* was scattered along the shores of Forteau Bay.

In 1939, the St. John's *Daily News* reported in its August 23rd edition that Captain Hounsell of the S.S. *Northern Ranger* had reported seeing a great amount of scrap iron along the north-shore side of the Straits of Belle Isle. The captain also reported bringing back to St. John's three huge pieces of solid brass from the *Raleigh's* condenser. Each piece weighed approximately one ton and fetched one hundred dollars in the scrap market.

That was the last official salvage from the *Raleigh*. Today the shattered hull lies in about fifteen feet of water. Except for the occasional bit of scrap washed ashore after a severe storm, the only reminder to a modern day visitor to the area of this wreck is the stone monument in the cemetery at L'Anse Amour. It has engraved on it the names of the unfortunate seamen who were drowned when the boat capsized in attempting to land the lifeline. They were as follows:

First Class Stoker, Herbert Bashford.
First Class Stoker, Silas Field.
First Class Stoker, George Fisher.
First Class Stoker, George M. Thornhill.
Petty Officer Stoke, Edward Effard,
Petty Officer Stoke, John E. Lloyd.
Leading Stoke, Sidney G. Tripp
Leading Stoke, Reuben Tyler
Able Seaman, Patrick Pattee.
Able Seaman, James Weaver.

Chapter 12

"REMEMBER THE *CARIBOU*"
October 13, 1942

In 1939, when Great Britain declared war on Germany, Newfoundland, as a British Crown Colony, was also at war with that nation. However in the first months of the war there was little or no enemy activity in and around the coastal waters of Newfoundland. Then came the "Battle of the Atlantic," and enemy submarine packs began to hunt the waters of the North Atlantic, seeking as their prey convoys from Canada and the United States bringing war materials and food to a beleaguered Britain.

Halifax and St. John's were the gathering points for many of these convoys, and as this became apparent to German intelligence, World War Two came to the coastal waters off Newfoundland and Nova Scotia. Many a fine ship left port only to fall prey to the torpedoes of the enemy submarines.

As Newfoundland had few roads to its many far flung outport settlements, the main connecting link for mail, freight and passengers service was the coastal marine service operated by the Newfoundland Government. As well, the government operated a scheduled ferry between Port aux Basques, Newfoundland, and Sydney, Nova Scotia, as part of this service. At the beginning of World War Two, the Newfoundland Government had ordered the ships of its marine service to observe certain special precautions, such as total black-outs while at sea, and urged the people to report any suspected enemy activity. As the intensity of enemy submarine activity increased in the North Atlantic, the Gulf ferry was sometimes accompanied for part of its way by a naval escort. Still, most Newfoundlanders did not take the threat of enemy action on the local coastal boats very seriously. The war still seemed a long way off in distant Asia and Europe.

It was a policy of the Newfoundland Marine Coastal Service that the flag-ship of the service should serve on the Gulf ferry service. In 1939, at the outbreak of hostilities, the S.S. *Caribou* was serving on this run.

This rare picture of the launching of the S.S. "Caribou" in July, 1925 shows well wishers admiring the boat. (Photo: Courtesy of Mr. Bren Kenney and Mr. Frank Graham).

The *Caribou* had been built in Holland especially for the Gulf Service in 1925. She was a comfortable, well appointed ship, especially designed for easy manoeuvring in the heavy ice which often plagued the Gulf run during early spring. The *Caribou* arrived at St. John's after her maiden voyage across the Atlantic on October twenty second, 1925. Following a few sea trials, she went into service on the Gulf, under the command of Captain L. Stevenson, an experienced Captain with the Newfoundland Marine Service.

For seventeen uneventful years the S.S. *Caribou* continued to make her tri-weekly run on her ninety-six mile voyage. Captain Stevenson retired from the *Caribou* and was replaced by Captain Britton, who in turn gave over his command to Captain Benjamin Taverner, and it was Captain Benjamin Taverner who commanded the *Caribou* on her last voyage.

The night of October 13th, 1942, was dark with no moon. The winds were light and the sea was calm. Wrapped in its war-time blackout, Sydney harbour was very quiet as the S.S. *Caribou* slipped her moorings and set out on her regular scheduled night crossing to Port aux Basques. At the beginning of the war, the management of the Newfoundland Railway had been opposed to night crossings on the Gulf run, but had been overruled by the naval authorities who insisted that the night crossings were necessary. On this particular night the naval authorities were aware that there were at least three German submarines operating in Canadian and Newfoundland coastal waters, but they did not change their policy regarding the necessity of the night crossings.

The authorities were also aware that the S.S. *Caribou* was listed in *Janes Fighting Ships,* as a reserve troop transport, and was therefore a legitimate target for an enemy attack.

On board for the October 13th crossing were two hundred thirty-seven people, made up of 46 regular crew members, 73 civilian passengers and 118 servicemen. The *Caribou* could accommodate 284 passengers and she carried life belts for 300 people. As she steamed quietly out of Sydney harbour in the early evening darkness, with Able Seaman John Dominie at the wheel, the *Caribou* was accompanied by the HMCS *Grandmere,* a Bangor class minesweeper. Meanwhile, outside Port aux Basques Harbour, the 500 ton German U-Boat 69, known to her crew as the "Laughing Cow" lay waiting for her prey.

The commander of U-69, Captain Lieutenant Ulrich Graf, shadowed the *Caribou* until she was about 40 miles from her destination, then gave the order to fire. Naval records of the day described the attack in this manner:

At 0240 hours, Atlantic Standard Time, the next morning (October 14th.) when the *Caribou* was about 40 miles south-west of her destination she was

63

struck by a torpedo on the starboard side, and sank in a few minutes. At the moment she was struck, HMSC *Grandmere* was on her starboard quarter and sighted the U-Boat on the surface ahead and to the starboard. She attempted to ram, but the submarine dived when she was still 150 yards off. As she passed ahead of the swirl left by the enemy, the *Grandmere* dropped a pattern of depth charges, but this counter-attack was probably inaccurate. She dropped two more patterns in the neighbourhood but was unable to locate the submarine by ASDIC.

In the meanwhile there was terror and panic on the sinking *Caribou*. Passengers awakened from their sleep by the explosion were running around in confusion. The lifeboats on the starboard side had been reduced to splinters by the explosion, and as the ship quickly filled with water the waves began to wash over her decks. Then the lights went out and within minutes the listing main deck on the starboard side was under water. In the darkness, and with floods of water rushing down the main stairways, it was impossible for the officers and crew of the *Caribou* to evacuate the passengers in an orderly manner, but Captain Taverner and his men did their best to do so as quickly as possible. In the true tradition of the sea, Captain Taverner stayed with his ship trying to keep her afloat as long as possible to give those under his care a chance to escape. He, together with his two sons who were junior officers, stewardess Bride Fitzpatrick and 31 other crew members went down with the ship.

There was a mad scramble to man the lifeboats and liferafts, and as the boats and rafts on the starboard side had been destroyed, all rushed to the port lifeboat stations. As a result of the general panic so many people crowded into number 4 lifeboat that it capsized due to overloading, throwing all into the icy waters. Number 2 lifeboat got away with just a few people in it, but later managed to pick up approximately 40 survivors from the water. The *Caribou* filled and sank so quickly that it was impossible to launch numbers 5 and 6 lifeboats. However, most of the liferafts floated free and a number of the passengers and crew were able to climb on these before the ship sank. It is estimated by the survivors that the *Caribou* sank within five minutes of the torpedo attack.

Although there was collective terror and panic there were also individual deeds of heroism, as in the case of Elizabeth Northcott of Burgeo, who while swimming for a liferaft, saw that the mother of 15 month old Leonard Shiers could no longer hold him. She reached out, took the baby and swam with him to a liferaft. Another story is told of the heroism of F/O Jack O'Brien who rescued two small infants by tucking them inside his Air Force greatcoat.

In the darkness and fearing another submarine attack, the HMCS *Grandmere* was unable to rescue survivors until the following morning.

Picture of the S.S. "Caribou" before it was sunk by a German Submarine on October 13, 1942. (Photo: Courtesy of Dr. Bobbie Robertson, Secretary, Newfoundland Historical Society)

During the night three liferafts stayed close together. There was not room for all the survivors on these rafts, and some had to remain in the water holding on to ropes trailing from the liferafts. Numb with the cold of the chilling waters they waited for morning and rescue. To keep up their spirit the survivors recited the Lord's Prayer and sang hymn after hymn, asking God's assistance to sustain them until their rescue. It was a long night, but at last the morning broke, and hope was rekindled when they saw aircraft flying by. Then at 8:30 a.m. their escort of the previous night, HMCS *Grandmere,* arrived and began to pick up the survivors on the liferafts. She took on board 103 survivors, some of whom were in desperate condition. Two died on their way back to Sydney. Before the *Grandmere* left to return to Sydney, two other armed yachts, the *Rainbow* and the *Elk* took up the search for other possible survivors.

When the final rescue had been made and all survivors accounted for, it was found that 137 people had died in the tragic sinking. Of those rescued 30 had suffered injuries and 8 had to be hospitalized. Only one of the *Caribou's* officers survived. He was Mr. Thomas Fleming, the ship's purser. In order to mark the heroism and devotion to duty shown by the officers and crew of the S.S. *Caribou,* 31 of whom had died during the sinking of their ship, the Railway Employees Welfare Association raised funds to erect a permanent memorial in Port aux Basques to their memory. One who was instrumental in having this memorial erected was Mr. James V. Ryan, the Assistant General Manager of the Newfoundland Railway at that time and president of the R.E.W.A.

The sinking of the S.S. *Caribou* brought the horror of World War Two home to every Newfoundlander. In the Channel-Port aux Basques area there were 21 widows and 51 orphans left as a result of the sinking. Immediately special measures were taken to protect the coastal fleet of the Newfoundland Railway. Each ship was equipped with a stern gun, and a naval officer, in order to repel further submarine attacks.

The wisdom of this move was seen some time later when the S.S. *Burgeo,* which had replaced the *Caribou,* on the Gulf run, was attacked by a German U-Boat. The *Burgeo* was able to dodge the torpedo, and the accurate aim of her gunner forced the U-Boat to submerge. Under water the submarine could not match the speed of the *Burgeo,* and the deadly fire from the stern gun kept her from surfacing. (It is said that when the captain of the *Burgeo* gave the order "full speed ahead", the chief engineer sat on the safety valve of the boiler, and the *Burgeo* increased her speed by several knots. The *Burgeo* made it safely to Port aux Basques, but because of the censorship of the time, the story was not publicized for fear of frightening the people.)

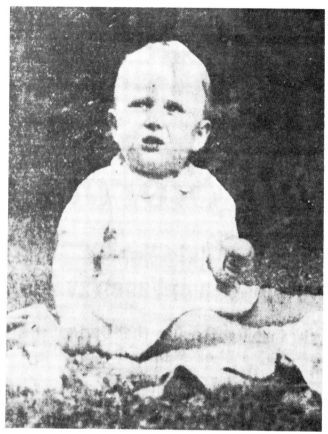

Leonard Shiers at age 15 months. He was rescued when the "Caribou" was sunk. (Photo: Courtesy of the Evening Telegram, October, 1942.)

The sinking of the *Caribou* also caused Newfoundlanders to redouble their war effort. At War Bond sales and recruiting drives, "Remember the *Caribou*" was a slogan that brought out pocket-books and recruited young men for duty overseas.

The war ended, and the sinking of the *Caribou,* like many other wartime events slowly faded from memory. Newfoundland became a part of Canada, and the Canadian National Railway replaced the Newfoundland Railway. New, larger ships replaced the *Burgeo* and the *Baccalieu* on the Gulf run: the *William Carson,* the *Patrick Morris,* the *Ambrose Shea,* and the *Frederick Carter.*

Then in imitation of the old Newfoundland Railway, the C.N.R. decided to build a very special ship for the Gulf run. It was to be the largest ferry ever built in Canada, at a total cost of 121 million dollars. Among the brass of the C.N.R. some dim memory stirred of another ferry built in 1925 for the same run, and once again a proud new *Caribou* was commissioned to be the company's flagship on the Gulf.

In order to honour the memory of the passengers and crew of the S.S. *Caribou* on her final voyage of 44 years before, C.N. Marine invited 14 survivors from that aborted crossing to sail on the maiden voyage of the M.V. *Caribou.* On May 13th, 1986 the M.V. *Caribou* sailed from North Sydney, and at 5:00 a.m. Captain Williams gave orders to cut the engines near the place where the ill-fated S.S. *Caribou* had gone down 44 years before. It was a very emotional moment for all on board (and especially for the survivors of that long ago voyage) when Mr. Mack Piercey of Fortune, a former member of the Royal Navy and survivor of the sinking, dropped a wreath overboard in memory of those who had paid the supreme sacrifice so long ago.

Appendix A

NEWFOUNDLANDERS WHO PERISHED IN THE WRECK OF THE
S.S. GEORGE WASHINGTON, ON OR ABOUT JAN. 20, 1877

ARCHIBALD W.
COMBER W. S.
FALCONER A.
HOPKINS JOHN
NEWBERRY WILLIAM
POWER JAMES
RAYNOR EDWARD

NAMES OF THOSE WHO DIED IN THE *GREENLAND* DISASTER
OF MARCH 1898.
(BODIES RECOVERED)

NAME	AGE	TOWN
COURAGE ARCHIBALD	30	HR. GRACE
CURTIS HENRY	23	NEWTOWN
DAVIS EDWIN	19	SAFE HR.
GREEN ISAAC	20	NEWTOWN
HEATH WILLIAM	22	HR. GRACE
HOUSE FREDERICK	18	GOOSEBERRY ISLAND
HOWELL JAMES	—	POOL'S ISLAND
HUNT EDWIN	18	CAPE FREEL'S ISLAND
KELLOWAY WILLIAM	48	POOL'S ISLAND
MAHER JAMES	18	QUIDI VIDI
MURPHY WALTER	34	CARBONEAR
NEWTRY ALFRED	18	CARBONEAR
NORRIS GEORGE	31	NEWTOWN
NORRIS WALTER	24	NEWTOWN

OSMOND JOSEPH	19	POOL'S ISLAND
PARSONS KENNETH	28	NEWTOWN
PINSENT JOHN	38	SAFE HR.
POND JACOB	20	GREENSPOND
PYNN RICHARD	19	ST. JOHN'S
RALPH CHARLES	22	FLAT ISLAND B.B.
THOMAS JOHN	40	POOL'S ISLAND
VINCENT JOHN	30	CAPE ISLAND
VOISEY WILLIAM	23	QUIDI VIDI
WHITE THOMAS	40	POOL'S ISLAND
WOOLRIDGE WILLIS	19	TRINITY

(BODIES NOT RECOVERED)

ANDREWS ALEX	21	CAPE ISLAND
BLACKWOOD WILLIAM	21	GREENSPOND
BOWLAN ALBERT	21	POUND COVE
BROWN BENJAMIN	22	POOL'S ISLAND
BUNGAY GEORGE	26	NEWTOWN
CHEEKS JAMES	40	NEWTOWN
CONWAY JACOB	27	TURK'S COVE
CULLEN WILLIAM	27	TORBAY
HENNESSEY NICHOLAS	30	ST. BRENDAN'S, B.B.
LARDER WILLIAM	26	TRINITY
MALLARD JAMES	24	ST. JOHN'S
MORTIMER NOAH	40	HR. GRACE
NORRIS HERBERT	24	NEWTOWN
NORRIS THEODORE	21	POUND COVE
PELLEY GEORGE W.	22	HANT'S HR.
PYNN GEORGE	27	HR. GRACE
RICKETTS THOMAS	35	KING'S COVE
ROGERS AMBROSE	22	LOWER ISLAND COVE
RYAN HEBER	23	SHIP'S COVE
SQUIRES STEPHEN	28	SALVAGE
WELLS LORENZO	34	HR. GRACE
WELLS MATTHEW	21	HR. GRACE
WICKS JOHN	34	WESLEYVILLE

NAMES AND PLACES OF RESIDENCE OF THE CREW OF THE S.S.
SOUTHERN CROSS MARCH 31, 1914

SEALERS

BATTON JAMES	FOXTRAP
BARRETT ED.	TILTON
BARRETT THOMAS	SPANIARD'S BAY
BARTLETT THOMAS	TURK'S GUT
BENSON ARTHUR	HR. GRACE
BISHOP JOHN	KELLIGREWS
BLUNDON JAMES	LOW POINT, C.B.
BOLAND JOHN	ST. JOHN'S
BRADBURY JOHN	HR. GRACE
BRAY JAMES	HR. GRACE
BRAY HERBERT	HR. GRACE
BRIGHT THOMAS	BREEN'S COVE
BURKE PAT	COLLIERS
BUSSEY JAMES	KELLIGREWS
BUSSEY JOS.	KELLIGREWS
BUSSEY NOAH	FOXTRAP
BUSSEY ALFRED	FOXTRAP
BUSSEY THOMAS	FOXTRAP
BUSSEY GORDON	FOXTRAP
BUTLER HENRY	FOXTRAP
BUTLER HERB	CUPIDS
BUTLER SAM	KELLIGREWS
BUTLER W. C.	FOXTRAP
BUTLER WILLIAM	KELLIGREWS
BUTLER W. J.	KELLIGREWS
BUTTON URIAH	KELLIGREWS
CALLAHAN JOHN	HR. GRACE
CARROL WALTER	OUTER COVE
CHAFE J.	PETTY HR.
CHAPMAN GEORGE	SPANIARD'S BAY
CHETMAN NATHAN	SPANIARD'S BAY
CLARKE ALBERT	PARADISE
CLARKE ART	SPANIARD'S BAY
CLARKE HY.	CARBONEAR
CLARKE JOHN	BRIGUS
CLARKE JOHN W.	PARADISE
CLARKE ROBERT	SPANIARD'S BAY
CLARKE WALTER	ST. JOHN'S

CLARKE WILLIAM	SPANIARD'S BAY
COLE ED.	COLLIERS
COLE JOHN	COLLIERS
CONWAY JOHN	COLLIERS
COMBER JOHN	ISLAND COVE
COOMBS WILLIAM	HR. GRACE
CORBETT JOS.	CLARKE'S BEACH
COSTELLO JOHN	CONCEPTION HR.
COSTELLO THOMAS	CONCEPTION HR.
CRANE ED.	SPANIARD'S BAY
DUNPHY JAMES	TORS COVE
DYER PAT	LOGY BAY
EBBS JOHN	ST. JOHN'S
ELLIS JOHN	ST. JOHN'S
EVANS JOHN	TORBAY
FIELD ALEX	TORBAY
FIELD JOHN	ST. JOHN'S
FOLLETT FRED	BROAD COVE
FOLEY JAMES	GREY ISLANDS
FORWARD OSCAR	CARBONEAR
FRENCH GEORGE	HARBOUR GRACE
GIBBONS ED.	ST. VINCENT'S
GIBBONS LAWRENCE	ST. VINCENT'S
GIBBONS SEBASTIAN	ST. VINCENT'S
GIBBONS THOMAS	ST. VINCENT'S
GILLET ROBERT	CARBONEAR
GOSSE ROBERT	SPANIARD'S BAY
GOSSE WILLIAM	SPANIARD'S BAY
GOSSE WILLIAM	LITTLE BAY
GRIFFIN JOHN	HR. GRACE
HALL GEORGE	COLLIERS
HANNON JOHN	BAY DE VERDE
HARRIS ABNER	ADEYTOWN
HEARN PAT	GOULDS
HICKEY THOMAS	HOLYROOD
HISCOCK GEORGE	TOPSAIL
HISCOCK JOHN P.	CARBONEAR
HOLLETT JAMES	ARNOLD'S COVE
HOWE WILLIAM J.	CARBONEAR
JAMES ELIAS	HR. GRACE
JAMES ISAAC	HR. GRACE
JAMES THOMAS	HR. GRACE

JAMES WILLIAM	HR. GRACE
JAMES W. C.	HR. GRACE
KEARNEY WILLIAM	SEAL COVE
KENNEDY SAMUEL	SEAL COVE
KENNY ED.	FERMEUSE
KNIGHT RONALD	HR. GRACE
LANDRY JOHN	NEW CHELSEA, T.B.
LEARY HENRY	KELLIGREWS
LINDSAY ALLAN	ST. JOHN'S
LYNCH WALTER	PARADISE
MALEY JAMES	KELLIGREWS
MANNING THOMAS	TORBAY
MANSFIELD JOHN	CONCEPTION HR.
MANSFIELD JOHN	ST. JOHN'S
MARTIN ARTHUR	HR. GRACE
MARTIN JAMES	ST. JOHN'S
MASON ELIAS	CATALINA
MATTHEWS AMBROSE	NEW CHELSEA, T.B.
MERCER JOHN	ISLAND COVE
MORRIS ELEAZER	CLARKE'S BEACH
MORRISSEY M.	HR. GRACE
MORGAN ALEC	SEAL COVE
MORGAN JOSEPH	SEAL COVE
MURRAY GEORGE	CARBONEAR
NEIL JAMES	ISLAND COVE
NEWEL FRED	UPPER ISLAND COVE
NEWEL JOSIAH	CARBONEAR
NEWELL MARTIN	UPPER ISLAND COVE
NORMAN CHARLES	CATALINA
NORMAN NOEL	HR. GRACE
NORMAN WILLIAM	CUPIDS
NOSEWORTHY ERNEST	HR. GRACE
NOSEWORTHY JAMES	HR. GRACE
O'ROURKE WALTER	OUTER COVE
PATRICK JAMES	CARBONEAR
PARSONS LORENZO	HR. GRACE
PARSONS WILFRED	HR. GRACE
PATRICK JAMES	CARBONEAR
PATTEN GEORGE	FOXTRAP
PENNY AMOS	CARBONEAR
PENNEY NORMAN	CARBONEAR
PENNEY ROBERT	CARBONEAR

PIERCE WALTER	CATALINA
PIKE ALFRED	CARBONEAR
PORTER JAMES	LONG POND, MANUELS
PYNN HERB	HR. GRACE
QUETEL CHARLES	ST. JOHN'S
QUILTY JAMES	HORSE COVE
RIDEOUT SAMUEL	KELLIGREWS
ROBBINS BEN	LOWER ISLAND COVE
ROBBINS JOHN	ISLAND COVE
ROBERTSON JAMES	ST. JOHN'S
ROWE JACOB	CHANCE COVE, T.B.
ROWE NOAH	CHANCE COVE
SHARP AMBROSE	PARADISE
SHARP WILLIAM	PARADISE
SKIFFINGTON LEONARD	NEWMAN'S COVE, B.B.
SMITH GEORGE	SPANIARD'S BAY
SMITH HENRY	MANUELS
SQUIRES ALEX	TOPSAIL
SQUIRES ED.	TOPSAIL
SQUIRES FRED	ST. JOHN'S
STANLEY JOHN	LOND POND, MANUELS
STANLEY WILLIAM	LONG POND, MANUELS
SPARKES NOAH	BRIGUS
SPARKES THOMAS	BRIGUS
TAYLOR AMBROSE	FOXTRAP
TAYLOR KENNETH	CUPIDS
VOKEY ISAAC	SPANIARD'S BAY
VOKEY GEORGE	SPANIARD'S BAY
VOKEY WILLIAM	SPANIARD'S BAY
WALSH JAMES	CONCEPTION HR.
WALSH JAMES	ST. VINCENT'S
WALSH JOHN	COLLIERS
WALSH WILLIAM	NORTHERN BAY
WATTS B.	BRIGUS
WEBBER WILLIAM	HR. GRACE
WHITE WILLIAM	ST. MARY'S
WINSOR ANGUS	BRIGUS
YEO LAWRENCE	ST. JOHN'S
YETMAN JOS.	SPANIARD'S BAY
YETMAN MARK	HR. GRACE
YOUDEN JAMES	BRIGUS

SHIP'S OFFICERS AND CREW, MARCH 1914

MASTER, GEORGE CLARK, BRIGUS
2ND HAND, JAMES KELLY, BRIGUS
CHIEF ENGINEER, DAVID PARSONS, ST. JOHN'S
2ND. ENGINEER, THOMAS CONNELL, ST. JOHN'S
3RD. ENGINEER, W. HAMMOND, ST. JOHN'S
FIREMAN, W. WALSH, ST. JOHN'S
FIREMAN, M. SCAMMELL, ST. JOHN'S
FIREMAN, P. STAPLETON, ST. JOHN'S
FIREMAN, GREGORY BREMNAN, ST. JOHN'S
FIREMAN, JOHN WHELAN, ST. JOHN'S

Appendix B

SOME NEWFOUNDLAND AND LABRADOR SHIPWRECKS

Abbeymoor, SS. Wrecked on Renews Rock 16 Oct 1896.

Acis, SS. Wrecked off Cape Race 3 Aug 1901.

Adamant. Driven from her anchors at Cat Harbour 18 Oct 1868. Captain John Munn and four others drowned.

Adelaide Falquet. French vessel found icebound in Placentia Bay with the frozen bodies of three men and one woman aboard. 4 Jan 1879.

Administratrix, MV. Sailed out of Grand Bank, Captain Chesley Forsey master. Lost with all hands 29 Apr 1948 after colliding with a Norwegian freighter.

Agnes J. Ryan. Freighter, sank near Botwood 28 Sept 1962.

Algerine. Sealing steamer, lost at Pond's Inlet 15 July 1912.

Alice Marie. French vessel wrecked at Clam Cove, near Cape Race 22 Sept 1887. Crew of eight men drowned, only survivor "Rionne", a young boy.

Alma. Schooner, sailed out of Scilly Cove (Winterton), Trinity Bay. Captain Piercey and a crew of six lost on Triton Island 14 Oct 1907.

Amberton, SS. British freighter, lost at St. Shotts 24 July 1947.

Andrews. Sailed out of Port de Grave. Lost on Biscayan Rock, Cape St. Francis 14 Oct 1840. Captain Andrews' son, daughter and one crew member died.

Anglo-Saxon, SS. Lost at Clam Cove near Cape Race 27 Apr 1863. 237 passengers and crew died.

Annie Healey. Schooner, sailed out of Fox Harbour, Placentia Bay. Lost with a crew of seven 25 Aug 1927. In this storm six schooners were lost along the south coast, with a total of 39 lives lost. Another two bank fishermen were killed when swept overboard by this storm.

Annie Jean. Schooner, sailed out of Isle aux Morts. Lost with all hands

25 Aug 1927. (see *Annie Healey*)

Annie Roberts. Schooner, sailed out of Lamaline. Sunk at Sydney, NS 22 Oct 1913. Five men drowned.

Antoinette. Schooner, sailed out of Harbour Grace. Lost with six men 30 Mar 1915.

Anton van Driel, SS. Lost with all hands, St. Shott's 29 Dec 1919.

Arbela, SS. Wrecked at St. Shott's with a cargo of lumber 10 June 1898.

Arctic, SS. Sunk after colliding with another vessel off Cape Race 27 Sept 1854.

Arctic Explorer. Research vessel, sank 3 July 1981 off St. Anthony. Lost were 13 of a crew of 21.

Argo, SS. Lost near Trepassey 28 June 1859.

Armistice. Schooner, Captain J. Petite master. Foundered mid-Atlantic 4 Jan 1923. Crew rescued by the SS *Horner City* and brought to Wales.

Assyrian, SS. Lost at Cape Race 5 June 1901.

Avalon. Brig, sank at the North Battery, St. John's Harbour 1 Feb 1848.

Avalon. Brig, lost on the rocks near Cape Ballard 2 Feb 1886.

Barracudina. Trawler, capsized in the Cabot Strait 26 Nov 1978. Crew of five drowned.

Begonia. Brig, left Twillingate Dec 1904 with six men and one woman on board. Never heard from again.

Belle of Burgeo. Schooner, lost with all hands on Sambro Ledge 7 Sept 1918.

Beothic, SS. Wrecked after running aground near Griquet 8 Dec 1940. Captain Stanley Barbour and crew safely landed.

Bessie Macdonald. Schooner, sailed out of Burin. Two crewmen lost after she capsized while fishing the Grand Banks 2 June 1924.

Betsy. Schooner, wrecked on the South Head of the Narrows. Captain Mainwaring and one crew member drowned 16 Dec 1811.

Betty. Galley, bringing winter supplies from London to Fort Frederick, Placentia. Lost off Trepassey 19 Oct 1721.

Beverley, SS. Missing with 22 crew members since she left Harbour Grace for Gibraltar 21 Jan 1918.

Bloodhound, SS. Second sealing steamer of that name, lost off Point L'Haye, St. Mary's Bay 15 July 1917.

Blossom. Schooner, Captain Joseph March. Wrecked at Gull Island, off Cape St. John 15 Sept 1891. Only one crew member survived.

Blue Mist II. Side trawler, owned by the Bonavista Cold Storage Company. Presumably sank off the southwest coast after experiencing problems with icing up 21 Feb 1966. Crew of 13 died.

Blue Wave. Side trawler, foundered on the Grand Banks on or about 10 Feb 1959. Lost were Captain Charles Walters and a 16 man crew.

Bluejacket, SS. Steam packet, destroyed by fire and explosion, Conception Bay 17 Sept 1862.

Bonavista, SS. Wrecked at Briar Point, N.S. 5 Mar 1912.

Bonne Bay, MV. Railway ship, wrecked at St. Shott's 20 Jan 1947.

Bonnie Lass. Schooner, lost with all hands off Trepassey 24 Sept 1916.

Bright Eye. Longliner, sank near Catalina 25 May 1954. Captain Little's son drowned.

Brithjof, SS. Norwegian ship lost at Cape Ballard, Renews 2 Jan 1885.

Brothers. Schooner, sailed out of Brigus. Lost in Baccalieu Tickle with 28 men on her way to the seal hunt 18 Mar 1823.

Burgeo, MV. Coastal boat, ran aground on Peckford's Island, near Fogo 6 July 1962.

Cacouna, SS. Lost off Ferryland Head 26 Sept 1914.

Cape Freels. Sank after catching fire 12 Mar 1976. Crew took to lifeboats and were rescued by the coast guard after 12 hours in the water.

Caribou, SS. Newfoundland Railway gulf ferry, sunk by enemy action 13 Oct 1942 with great loss of life.

Carranza. Schooner, sailed out of Pushthrough, Captain J. Matthews master. Sank after being split by lightning off Scaterie 18 Sept 1930. Schooner *Vignette* rescued six crewmen, 10 lost. In the fall of 1930 there were several other casualties from severe lightning storms; three fishermen were lost off Lumsden when their boat was struck, a Pouch Cove man was killed by a lightning bolt while out walking and a St. John's man died by lightning while phoning his wife.

Carrie and Evelyn. Schooner, sailed out of Hant's Harbour. All hands lost when wrecked at Fox Holes, Torbay 25 Aug 1935. All told 20 fishermen were lost in this August gale.

Centaurius. Schooner, sailed out of Denmark. Left Harbour Buffett for Oporto 7 Feb 1923, never seen again. The crew was at a definite disadvantage, for they were sailing without their captain who was under arrest for shooting one of his crew.

Christabel. Barque, wrecked off Bonavista 7 June 1885. Crew rescued through the bravery of three Bonavista men.

Christmas Seal. Burned and sank off Nova Scotia 13 May 1976. This vessel was for many years a floating X-ray clinic in Newfoundland waters.

Cleopatra, SS. Lost off Cape Race 8 Aug 1860.

Clintonia. Schooner, sailed out of Belleoram, Captain Healey master. Wrecked while bound for Halifax 12 Oct 1924. Crew was picked up in the water by the *Emperor of Scotland* and brought to New York.

Columbine. Schooner, sailed out of Stone's Cove, Fortune Bay, Captain J. Tibbo. Lost at Belloram with five men 18 Nov 1905.

Czar. Schooner, sailed out of Carbonear. Lost at the Funks with four men 8 June 1901.

Dantzig. Schooner, sailed out of Fortune. Sank off Cape Breton Island, crew rescued 26 Nov 1953.

Del Ray. Longliner, abandoned after catching afire in Placentia Bay 27 July 1972. Only six of her crew of 15 were rescued.

Delano, SS. Lost at Seal Cove, Renews 14 Aug 1902.

Delmar, SS. Wrecked near Cape Ballard, Renews 8 July 1901.

Derville, SS. Left Emily Harbour, Labrador with a load of fish 19 Oct 1925. Captain Havard and a crew of 15 never heard of again.

Discovery. Schooner, lost at Broad Cove, Bonavista Bay 18 Oct 1869.

Donald L. Silver. Schooner, sailed out of Gloucester, Mass. Wrecked on the West Coast after collecting a load of herring in the Bay of Islands 4 Jan 1924. Six drowned.

Dora. Brigantine, lost at Petty Harbour 7 May 1875.

Douala. French freighter, sank 20 Dec 1963. Picked up in lifeboats were 17 of her crew of 29.

Dove. Schooner, belonging to S March and Sons, Old Perlican. Lost with 23 persons on board 20 May 1871.

Drake, HMS. Lost at St. Shott's, 13 drowned 23 June 1822.

Duchess of Fife. Reid Newfoundland Co. steamer, lost at Lance Cove 19 Sept 1907.

Dundee, SS. Reid Newfoundland Co. coastal steamer, wrecked at Noggin Island, Gander Bay 26 Dec 1919.

Dundannah. Schooner, lost with all hands while sealing in the Gulf 18 Mar 1872.

Durango, SS. Torpedoed by an enemy submarine 1917.

D.V. Chipman. Bark, lost with Captain Garland and three of his crew 18 June 1879.

Eagle, SS. Lost while whaling 15 Sept 1893.

Earle Monsport. Schooner, sailed out of Carbonear. Foundered 17 Jan 1948. Crew saved.

Edward. Schooner, missing with crew of six after leaving St. John's for King's Cove 16 Dec 1876.

Effie M. Schooner, lost at Great Brook near Old Perlican 19 Sept 1907. Master and all 16 crew killed. It was reported that over 90 vessels were wrecked or driven ashore in this storm.

Eleanor. Schooner, Captain E. Kinsella. Ran ashore near Witless Bay, crew all saved 11 Jan 1923.

Electric. Schooner, lost at Point Lance with two men 4 Feb 1861.

Elfrida. Brig, Captain Jeffers. Lost at Mosquito Point with 4,000 seal pelts aboard. Nine crewmen drowned 18 Apr 1869.

Eliza. Brig, lost at Bay Bulls 23 Mar 1862.

Ella May. Schooner, sailed out of Rencontre West. Lost with all hands 25 Aug 1927 (see *Annie Healey*).

Elliot, SS. Lost at St. Paul's Inlet while sealing 22 Mar 1904.

Elsie Burdett. Schooner, Captain Cluett master. Lost with a crew of six 24 May 1917.

Emma. Brig, Captain White master. Ran ashore at Seal Cove, near Flat Rock 9 Nov 1856.

Emma M. Randolph. Schooner, sailed out of Shambler's Cove, Bonavista Bay, Captain Eleazer Blackwood master. Wrecked off North Head, Catalina 6 Dec 1926. Only the skipper's son survived out of a crew of nine.

Erik, SS. Sealing steamer torpedoed off Gallantry Head, St. Pierre 24 Aug 1916.

Erna, SS. Lost on a voyage from Glasgow, Scotland to St. John's with 51 persons on board, including survivors of the wrecked vessel *Aureola*. Cleared port 28 Feb 1912.

Ethie, SS. Wrecked at Martin's Point near Bonne Bay 11 Dec 1919.

Passengers and crew were saved when a local water dog brought a lifeline to the ship. A baby on board was brought to safety in a mailbag. Captain Edward English received a commendation from Governor Harris for his seamanship in averting a disaster.

Eubriom, SS. Belgian relief ship, wrecked at Cape Race 14 July 1917.

Evelyn. Schooner, wreckage sighted 8 May 1924. Presumed lost were five Newfoundlanders and three Danes.

Evelyn V. Miller. Schooner, wreck at Mall Bay, St. Mary's Bay with a load of oil for Imperial Oil. No loss of life. 26 Feb 1927.

Falcon, SS. Coastal mail steamer, lost at Isle au Bois, Ferryland 17 May 1851.

Ferryland, MV. Wrecked in the Caribbean, crew rescued 14 Feb 1953.

Fife. Reid Newfoundland Company steamer, sank Nov 1900 at St. John's Bay.

Finbarr. British factory trawler, sank 35 miles off St. Anthony with the loss of 12 lives 25 Dec 1966.

Fling. Schooner, lost off Holyrood (St. Vincent's), St. Mary's Bay 1880.

Florence. Schooner, collided with the Allan Line steamer *Scandanavian* off Cape Race 24 Apr 1897. Five killed.

Florence. Schooner, wrecked off St. Pierre 30 November 1940. Captain Arch Thornhill and his crew saved.

Florence, SS. Captain Barr master, lost at Mariner's Cove, St. Shott's 20 Dec 1912. Five survivors out of a crew of 25.

Florence. American brig, Captain Rose master. Lost at Cape Race 9 Aug 1840. Drowned were the first mate and 49 German immigrants on their way to New York.

Florizel, SS. Steamer of the Red Cross Line, wrecked near Renews 26 Feb 1918. Drowned were 94 passengers and crew.

Flying Cloud. Mail packet boat, Captain William Buffett master. Lost on the Fortune Bay run with her skipper and five crewmen 8 Mar 1862.

Francis P. Duke. Schooner, wrecked on Shag Rock, near Greenspond 17 Dec 1947. Captain William Miller and a crew of five Fogo men lost.

Francis Robie. Schooner, sailed out of the Bay of Islands. Captain Charles Benoit and four crewmen have not been seen since 4 Nov 1946.

Gabriella. Dutch freighter, abandoned by her 15 man crew in a raging storm 19 Oct 1976. All but two were drowned, with the second mate rescued by a Canadian Forces rescue specialist who dangled from a helicopter to pluck the mate from a lifeboat in 40 foot seas.

Garland. Sank after colliding with the *Golden Dawn* during a snow squall 10 Nov 1940. The "Tickle Disaster" killed 25 of the *Garland*'s 30 passengers, who were returning to Bell Island after a day in Portugal Cove.

Gem. Brig, three men killed when she burnt at Harbour Grace 12 Mar 1862.

George Foote. Banking schooner, sailing out of Grand Bank. Collided with another vessel while fishing the Grand Banks 22 Aug 1892. 17 men drowned.

George May. Schooner, Captain Downey master. Lost with the skipper, his wife and three children 13 Oct 1912.

George Washington, SS. Lost with all hands at Bristow Cove near Mistaken Point, Trepassey 20 Jan 1877.

Germania, SS. Lost near Cape Race 8 Aug 1869. Crew and passengers were saved by the heroic action of local resident Paddy Coombs who swam through the surf to bring a lifeline to the ship.

Gertie. Schooner, sailed out of Trepassey. Lost with all hands at Calvert 4 Dec 1934.

Gertrude, SS. Lost off Cape Pine 1886.

Grace Hall. Schooner, sailed out of Burgeo. Lost on the Grand Banks 26 Aug 1887 with Captain Burke and 11 crewmen.

Greenland, SS. Sank at the ice without loss of life Mar 1907.

Hanoverian, SS. Lost near Trepassey 31 Aug 1885.

Harcourt Kent,MS. Wrecked off Murrock Cove, St Shotts 22 Nov 1949. Crew of 14 men saved by residents of St Shotts who hauled the men over a 200 foot cliff.

Harlaw, SS. Lost while sealing in the Gulf 7 April 1911.

Harmony. Brig, Captain Bertram master. Lost at Duck Island near Rose Blanche 9 Dec 1868 returning from Cadiz. Only one of her crew of nine survived.

Haskel. Schooner, sailed out of Bonavista. Never heard of after leaving Griquet early Nov 1919.

Hawk, SS. Lost near Cape John 14 May 1876. Captain Arthur Jackman master.

Heather. Brig, lost in the ice off Cape Spear en route to St. John's from

Baltimore 24 Mar 1856. Captain Ash of Trinity and three others drowned.

Heligoland, SS. Oil tanker, lost with all hands at St. Shott's 11 Jan 1900.

Helen C. Morse. Schooner, lost with a crew of six. Wreckage picked up at Little Bay Islands 7 Nov 1921.

Helga. Bark, sailed out of Sweden. Ran ashore at Renews Island, of a 12 man crew only one escaped 2 May 1891.

Henry Stone, MV. Coaster, sank off Goose Bay 19 Nov 1959.

Herbert Warren. Schooner, given up as lost 19 June 1923.

Hercules. Fishing vessel, driven on the rocks at St. Mary's spring 1721.

Hercules. Mail steamer, burnt at Burin 19 Jan 1893.

Herder, SS. Wrecked at Long Beach near Trepassey 5 Oct 1882.

Hilda Gertrude. Schooner, sailed out of Rushoon, Placentia. Lost with all hands 25 Aug 1927 (see *Annie Healey*).

Hit or Miss. Schooner, lost in Notre Dame Bay with three men 29 Nov 1858.

Hope. Schooner, sailed out of Harbour Grace. Lost with 12 lives at White Bear Islands, Labrador in the great gale of 11-12 Oct 1885.

Hopewell. Schooner, sailed out of Harbour Main. Lost at Biscayan Rock, Cape St. Francis 29 Nov 1875. Seven people drowned and a man named Waugh escaped by clinging to the rock until the following day when he was rescued by the mail steamer *Hercules* (see above). This storm also wrecked the *Waterwitch*.

Humphrey John. Packet boat, lost in Conception Bay with skipper and all his passengers 7 Nov 1822.

Hungarian, SS. Lost with all hands about 150 miles off Cape Race 20 Feb 1860.

Huntsman. Brig, Captain R. Dawe of Bay Roberts master. Lost at the ice with 44 of her crew 23 April 1872.

Inez G. Schooner, sailed out of Burgeo, Captain Joseph Vatcher master. Lost with six crewmen after capsizing 26 Sept 1925.

Ingrahan, SS. Steam tug, lost at the Penguin Islands 5 Dec 1921. Crew Rescued.

Isabel. Brig, lost with all hands at Cape Race 27 Feb 1881.

J.H. Blackmore. Sealing steamer, lost off Cape Bonavista 9 Mar 1948.

James Spurrell. Ran ashore near Codroy while sealing in the Gulf 5 Apr

1954. Crew rescued.

Jeannie Barno. Coastal freighter, Captain Richard Penney. Missing and presumed lost 16 Aug 1960, on a voyage from Trepassey to St. John's.

Jemima. Schooner, lost with three drowned at Kelly's Island, Conception Bay 8 Aug 1864.

John and Maria. Schooner, lost at Brigus Head, Cape Broyle 2 Mar 1857. Of her crew of 26 only two escaped, Captain Carew and one boy.

John C. Loghlan. Schooner, sailed out of Red Harbour, Placentia Bay. Lost with her crew of seven 25 Aug 1927 (see *Annie Healey*).

John Knox, SS. Lost at Channel with 20 crewmen 3 May 1887. Captain Brolly master.

Julia A. Anderson. Lost with Captain Alex Chaisson and all hands. Some wreckage was discovered near Rose Blanche 27 Apr 1936.

Keltic, SS. Exploded and sank after a fire in the engine room 20 Dec 1949. The 11 man crew rowed a lifeboat to safety at Point Le Haye, St. Mary's Bay.

Kestre, SS. Lost at St. Shott's 22 July 1849. Captain Meagher master.

King. Western boat, lost at Cape St. Mary's with five men Aug 1892.

Kristioni, SS. Scandanavian passenger liner, lost west of Cape Race 14 July 1917.

Labrador, SS. Wrecked at Branch on her way to the Gulf seal hunt 15 March 1913.

Lady MacDonald. Sealer, crushed in ice and sank off Cape Norman 22 Mar 1951. Crew rescued by the *Linda May*.

Lady Sherbrooke. Passenger ship, lost with 268 persons near Cape Ray 19 July 1831. Rescued were Captain Gambles, two seamen and 27 passengers.

Langlecrag. Freighter, broke up and sank off Sacred Island, Pistolet Bay 15 Nov 1947. To illustrate the importance of radio to the modern ship wreck: the radio operator of the *Langlecrag* went back to the ship to recover the transmitter and maintain contact with rescuers. Within hours of the wreck a party set out overland from St. Anthony to provide assistance, Canadian and US coast guard vessels were steaming to the area and airplanes stood by in Goose Bay prepared to drop supplies to the survivors. There were two killed out of a crew of 43, with the remainder rescued by a Norwegian whaler.

Lantana. Brig, lost on Shag Rock, St. Mary's Bay with seven men 4 Jan

1891.

Latona. Longliner, sailed out of Englee. Crushed by ice and sank off Gannet Island, Labrador 16 Mar 1981. Crew rescued.

Laurentian, SS. A steamer of the Allan Line, lost at Mistaken Point, Trepassey 6 Sept 1909.

Lavinia. Bark, Driven on the rocks by ice at Seal Cove, Renews 18 Feb 1909. Crew all rescued.

La Violette. French vessel lost about 40 miles off Cape Pine 12 Mar 1875.

Lavrock. Church of England missionary ship lost off the west coast 9 July 1909.

Leaside. Longliner, crushed by ice and sank off Isle aux Morts 10 Mar 1966.

Leopard, SS. Sealing vessel, lost at Cape Ballard 6 May 1907.

Lillian. Schooner, lost near Grates Cove 14 Oct 1902. Drowned were Captain Martin's two sons and a girl named Ettie Campion.

Lily, HMS. Lost at Forteau, Labrador with seven of her crew 16 Sept 1889.

Lima. Schooner, Lost with her crew of five at Petty Harbour Motion 1 Jan 1853.

Lion, SS. Lost with all hands in Baccalieu Tickle 6 Jan 1882. Reported to have exploded.

Liseaux. Canadian freighter, foundered off the Newfoundland coast 27 Nov 1940. Ten men went down with the ship and twelve managed to board one of her lifeboats. The lifeboat was picked up 1 Dec, by which time two more had died of exposure.

Little Jap. Schooner, left Deer Island, Bonavista Bay 9 Nov 1909 with 13 people on board. Never a trace was found of her.

Little Princess. Schooner, belonging to the celebrated sealing captain Abram Kean. Abandoned in mid-ocean 1 Dec 1923.

Lizette, SS. Sunk while towing a vessel into Harbour Grace 16 Nov 1875.

Lizzie M. Stanley. Schooner, sailed out of Burgeo. Lost with a crew of six while en route to Catalina from St. Pierre 2 Jan 1881.

Lloyd Elsworth. Schooner, sailed out of Flat Islands, Bonavista Bay. Captain Lewis Samson and four crewmen drowned 23 May 1933 when a boat loaded with freight sank.

Lloydsen, SS. Wrecked at Channel en route to the Gulf seal hunt 10 Mar 1913.

Lois Jane. Schooner, left Emily Harbour, Labrador for Makkovic 17 Sept 1891. Never seen again, believed lost were a crew of six from Harbour Grace.

Lord Strathcona. Merchantman, sunk by German U-boat 513 at Bell Island 5 Sept 1942.

Louisburg, SS. Lost in St. Mary's Bay with a load of coal 5 May 1918.

Louise, SS. Wrecked at Indian Islands 13 May 1910.

Loyalist, SS. Lost at Freshwater Cove, Trepassey 28 Sept 1904.

Lucerne, SS. Left Ardrossan, Scotland 23 Jan 1901 with a load of coal for St. John's. Some wreckage was picked up in Conception Bay in February.

Lusitania, SS. Wrecked at Seal Cove, Renews 25 June 1901.

Madonna. Schooner, sailed out of Placentia. Broke up on Jude Island, near Oderin, Placentia Bay 1 Nov 1915. Two of her crew died of exposure.

Maggie. Schooner, sank after a collision with the steamer *Tiber* off the Narrows 7 Nov 1896. Drowned were thirteen crewmen.

Maggie Foote. Schooner, sank off Cape Pine 22 Aug 1892 with the loss of five men.

Magno. Schooner, lost during a hurricane while sailing from Sydney NS to Port aux Basques 17 Aug 1924. Captain Levi Baggs and four crewmen lost.

Magnolia. Schooner, sailed out of Brigus, Captain Piercey master. Wrecked at Freshwater Bay en Route to Brigus from Sydney NS with a load of coal 24 Dec 1872. Only one of the crew survived to see Christmas Day.

Marechale de Luxembourg. French banker, carried a crew of 40. Last sighted 18 May 1935.

Margaret K. Smith. Schooner, presumed lost after sailing out of Halifax 26 Aug 1943.

Maria. Bark, lost in St. George's Bay with four of her crew 11 Nov 1868. carrying a load of timber from Quebec to Liverpool.

Maria Joanna. Portuguese vessel, ran aground at the entrance to Fogo harbour. 28 Sept 1948.

Marian. Schooner, Captain Waddy master. Lost with a crew of 15 en route from St. John's to Change Islands 12 Nov 1859.

Marion. Banking schooner, sailed out of Fortune Bay, Captain Ike Jones master. Lost with 17 hands under mysterious circumstances 18 June 1915.

Mariposa, SS. Lost in the Strait of Belle Isle 24 Sept 1895.

Mary Ann. Schooner, sailed out of Northern Bay, Conception Bay. Sank after colliding with the schooner *Somerset* near the Sugar Loaf 24 Sept 1886. Four persons drowned.

Mary Pauline. Coastal freighter, lost off St. Pierre 20 Dec 1963, bound for Burin with a load of coal. All drowned but one of a seven man crew.

Mastiff, SS. Lost at the seal hunt in the spring of 1898.

Maud Thornhill. Lost with all hands 1 Feb 1929.

Mayaquzanna. Spanish brig, lost at Blackhead 14 Aug 1876. Captain and his wife drowned.

Meigle, SS. Wrecked at St. Shotts 19 July 1947.

Memento. Schooner, lost with all hands on Renews Rock 19 June 1873.

Minnie Parsons. Schooner, Captain Pierce Judge master. Lost in a gale in the Strait of Belle Isle.

Monasco. American bark, Captain A.F. Bailey master. Ran ashore about three miles west of Burin 21 July 1857. a total of 55 passengers were drowned.

Monica Hartery. Sailed out of Channel, Captain Alex Keeping master. Lost with all hands at Rose Blanche Point 24 Dec 1933.

Monico Walters. Crushed by ice while sealing in the Gulf 26 Mar 1948.

M.L. Truman. Schooner, lost at Mutton Bay, Trepassey with all hands except the Captain 28 March 1868.

Montpelier, SS. Lost at Gull Island near Channel 4 May 1900.

Morien, SS. left Louisburg 16 Nov 1912 with a load of coal for Placentia, but never reached port. In Sept 1922 the wreck of the ship was discovered at the bottom of St. Bride's harbour. Captain C.M. Burchell and a crew of 20 all presumed dead.

My Beauty. Schooner, foundered while en route to St. John's from Sydney 28 Aug 1905. All hands lost.

Myers Three. Longliner, sank off Codroy 24 Jan 1987. Five drowned.

Naomi. Brig, lost at Outer Cove with all hands 18 Jan 1853.

Native Lass. Brigantine, never seen after sailing out of the Narrows 18 Jan 1847.

Nautilus. Brig, Captain Burke master. Lost at Petty Harbour Motion with her skipper, his son and three crewmen 1 Jan 1865.

Newfoundlander, MV. Crushed in the ice while sealing 18 Mar 1954. Crew rescued.

Niobe, HMS. Wrecked on Great Miquelon 21 Mar 1874.

Nordhavet. Danish freighter, sunk off Cape St. Mary's 23 Sept 1945.

Norma Marilyn. Banker, lost near St. Shott's 4 May 1947. Crew rescued.

Norman W. Strong. Schooner, sailed out of Little Bay Islands, Captain Wiseman master. Lost with all hands off Castle Hyde, near Little St. Lawrence 2 Oct 1923.

Ocean Friend. Schooner, sailed out of Carbonear, Captain Penney master. Lost on the Grand Banks with a crew of 14, 15 Sep 1887.

Ocean Ranger. Semi-submersible oil exploration platform, sank on the Hibernia oilfield 175 miles east off St. John's 15 Feb 1982. None of her crew of 84 survived.

Octavia. Barquentine, Captain Disney master. Wrecked near Ferryland 6 Aug 1883. Crew saved through the heroic actions of Philip Keough, who was later presented with a silver medal by Sir Frederick B.T. Carter on behalf of the Royal Humane Society.

Orion. Schooner, sailed out of Grand Bank. Lost 5 Oct 1907 on the northeast coast. This one wreck orphaned 31 children in her home port.

Palestrina, SS. Lost at Bay Bulls 15 Oct 1896.

Panther, SS. Lost while sealing at the Front 22 Mar 1908.

Paradise. Western boat, wrecked while attempting to enter the Narrows on North Head 4 Dec 1811. Five passengers drowned, including two women and a young girl.

Parsee. Schooner, Captain J.C. Kean master. Lost at the Funks with eight men 15 Sept 1891.

Partanna. Banking schooner, sailed out of Grand Bank, Captain Anstey master. Crew of 25 lost when she came ashore at Drook, near Cape Race 5 May 1936.

Pascal and Annie. Ferry, wrecked and abandoned off St. Pierre 3 Nov 1970.

Patrick Morris, MV. Sank about 10 miles off the northern tip of Cape Breton Island 20 Apr 1970, while engaged in a search for a Newfoundland trawler crew. The captain and three engineers went down with the ship.

Passport. Schooner, sailed out of Greenspond. Lost at Caplin Cove, Conception Bay 5 Dec 1921. Nine drowned.

Peary, MV. Sailed out of Fortune, sank west of Burin 23 Aug 1961. Crew saved.

Pollux, SS. American naval freighter, ran ashore near St. Lawrence 10 Feb 1942. (see *Truxton*)

President Coaker. Schooner, sailed out of Port Union. Lost with all hands off Shoe Cove, Cape Ballard 1 Feb 1924.

Princess. Packet boat, lost with four men while plying her regular route between Portugal Cove and Harbour Grace 9 Sept 1850.

Pubnico Belle. Schooner. Among those lost at Baccalieu Tickle 8 July 1891 were two women and five children.

Puritan. Schooner, wrecked at Puffin Island 26 Dec 1899. Only one of a crew of eight survived.

R.L. Borden. Schooner, sank at Deadman's Cove, Hermitage 18 Dec 1929.

Rafaela. Spanish vessel wrecked at Long Beach, Cape Race 31 Aug 1876.

Raleigh, HMS. British light cruiser, ran ashore at Point Amour, Labrador 8 Aug 1922. Eleven men died.

Ravenal. Trawler, sailed out of St. Pierre. Wreckage recovered 31 Jan 1962 near Lories, Burin Peninsula. Presumed lost with all hands.

Reason. Schooner, sailed out of Placentia. Lost with 12 men in a tremendous gale 22 Aug 1892.

Regulus, SS. Sank with 20 men at Petty Harbour Motion 23 Oct 1910.

Release. Schooner, sailed out of Small Point, Conception Bay. Lost at White Bear Islands, Labrador with several families aboard returning from the Labrador fishery. One of many lost during the great gale of 11-12 Oct 1885. A total of 27 died, including many women and children, on the *Release* alone.

Renews. Richard Rose master. Capsized while entering Renews Harbour 10 Aug 1815. Six men drowned out of a crew of ten.

Rimouski, SS. Lost near Louisburg NS 9 Jan 1900.

Robert Frampton. Schooner, sailed out of Port aux Basques. Presumed lost with a crew of four 3 Dec 1945.

Rose. Schooner, sailed out of Spaniard's Bay. Sank with 12 aboard after striking an ice pan off La Scie 17 June 1894.

Rose. Schooner, sailed out of Carbonear, Captain James Kennedy master. Sailed out of Assiz Harbour, Labrador after a successful voyage at the Labrador fishery 15 Oct 1877. Ship and 37 passengers and crew lost.

Rosecastle. Freighter, sunk at Bell Island by a German U-boat 2 Nov 1942.

Roy Bruce. Schooner, sailed out of Burin, R.F. Hollett master. Missing since 15 Jan 1924 with a crew from Burin and Grand Bank.

Russell Lake. Schooner, sailed out of Fortune, Captain Frank Stoodley master. Lost with a crew of Five 17 Mar 1928.

Saganaga. Sunk at Bell Island by a German U-boat 5 Sept 1942.

St. Richard. Trawler, capsized and sank on the Grand Banks 1 Jan 1951. Crew rescued, apart from cook, who died of a heart attack.

Salmah. Brig, lost at Cape Spear 17 Nov 1861. Three men drowned.

Sandbeach, SS. Lost with all hands off St. George's. Some bodies were recovered 6 Dec 1932.

Sanseimo. French vessel lost on Caplin Rock 7 Aug 1874. No loss of life.

Schenk Caroline. Brigantine, lost at Petty Harbour Motion 3 Oct 1860.

Seaforth Jarl. Supply ship, wrecked off St. Pierre 18 Dec 1983. Crew rescued after taking to lifeboats.

Shamrock. Sailed out of St. Mary's. Lost with all hands at Cape St. Mary's 19 Sept 1846.

Siegfried. Schooner, lost with her crew of five at Burnt Harbour Point, Ferryland 4 Dec 1903.

Sid and Sam. Coaster, sunk off Keels, Bonavista Bay 17 April 1955. Crew rescued.

Sir John Harvey. Brigantine, lost near Random Island 18 Oct 1855. Three men drowned out of a total of 82 on board.

Six Brothers. Schooner, left Lower Island Cove 10 May 1883 to cut firewood in Trinity Bay. Neither ship, nor 14 on board ever heard of again.

Slipweek. Western boat, sailed out of Bay Roberts, Captain Snow master. Lost at Biscayan Cove, near Cape St. Francis 10 Nov 1890.

Snorre. Norwegian vessel, lost at Bonavista with two of her crew 15 Sept 1907. Lewis Little of Bonavista was decorated by King Haakon of Norway and the Carnegie Foundation for acts of bravery in saving the lives of crewmen.

Snowbird. Schooner, left St. John's with a crew of five en route to La Haye, France 26 April 1894. Found capsized in St. Mary's Bay.

Southampton. Sailed out of London, England, Henry Lee master. Lost near Bay Bulls with four crewmen 5 Nov 1818.

Southern Cross, SS. Believed to have sunk on the night of 31 Mar 1914 while returning from the Gulf seal hunt.

Spray. Brig, lost at Torbay with nine men 1 May 1869.

Star. Lost at Grey River, east of Burgeo 18 July 1871. No loss of life.

Stella Maris. Schooner, wrecked at Stag Harbour Run 25 Jan 1887.

Strathcona, SS. Hospital ship, used by the International Grenfell Association along the Labrador coast. Foundered north of Seldom-Come-By 2 Oct 1922.

St. Patrick. Mail and passenger packet, lost with five aboard at Crocker's Cove Point en route to Carbonear from Portugal Cove 21 nov 1840.

Sunbeam. Schooner, sailed out of Harbour Grace 17 Sept 1884. Captain Lester and crew never heard of again.

Susan. Schooner, three men drowned after she collided with an iceberg off the Narrows 26 Mar 1887.

Susan. Barquentine, lost 28 Mar 1887 with a crew of five. A bad week for *Susan*'s.

Swallow. Schooner, sailed out of Pilley's Island, Captain F. Morris master. Lost at Long Island, New York with her crew of 10 men 15 Jan 1909.

Teaser. Crushed in the ice while sealing in the Gulf 26 Mar 1948.

Terra Nova. Sank 21 Mar 1964.

Tezeza. Fishing vessel out St. Malo, France lost at St. Mary's Bay spring 1721.

Thule. Brig, driven ashore near Port aux Basques 26 Sept 1839. Lost with all hands.

Tigress, SS. Sank after exploding at the seal hunt 2 April 1875, Captain T. Bartlett master. Most of the 21 crewmen lost were from the Bay Roberts area.

Titania. Iron bark, wrecked at Pound Cove, Trepassey 17 Nov 1901. One man killed.

Tolesby, SS. Captain J.S. Payne master. Wrecked at Freshwater Point, Trepassey Bay 14 Jan 1908.

Tormore, SS. Wrecked at Cuckhold Head, Trepassey Bay 15 Jan 1896. No loss of life.

Treasure. Schooner, sailed out of Brigus. Lost during Christmas week 1903 with six men on her way to Sydney NS.

Truxton. American naval destroyer, ran aground at Chambers Cove near St. Lawrence 18 Feb 1942. She was battered to pieces along with the *Pollux*. Although many were saved through the heroic actions of the people of St. Lawrence and Lawn, 203 died in the wrecks. A third ship, the *Wilkes* was able to work itself free.

Tweed, HMS. Sloop, Captain Mather and 60 officers and men lost at Bay Bulls 5 Nov 1813.

Tyre. Four crewmen of Lamaline washed overboard during a storm 25 Oct 1938. The engineer survived and later brought the vessel into St. Pierre.

Unicorn. Sailed for the ice from French Harbour 1 May 1834. Never heard of again.

Unicorn. Schooner, lost at Cat Harbour with two men 6 Oct 1859.

Union. Brig, Captain J. Delaney master. Sailed from Trinity 1 Mar 1834 with a crew of 35 on her first trip to the ice. Never heard from again.

Vibert T. Shave. Schooner, sailed out of Grand Bank. Only the skipper survived after she was rammed by the ore carrier *Haugarland,* 2 miles off Ferryland 27 Sept 1930.

Victoria. Packet boat, lost with a crew of four while making the trip from Portugal Cove to Harbour Grace, 9 Sep 1850.

Vienna. Schooner, sailed out of Burnt Islands. Lost with a crew of six during a terrific gale on the southwest coast 25 Aug 1927 (see *Annie Healey*).

Viking, SS. Blew up 15 Mar 1931. 25 killed, the remainder walked eight miles on the ice to the Horse Islands. Among the dead were US film-makers Varrick Frissell and A.E. Penrod, who had been making a movie about the seal hunt. The last of the great sealing disasters.

Village Belle. Captain John Antle master. Last seen when she set sail from Brigus in Mar 1872.

Virgin Lass. Brigantine, owned by P. Brown of Harbour Grace. Lost with all hands near Catherine's River NS 31 Oct 1845.

Walrus, SS. Lost at the ice 26 Mar 1908.

Warren M. Colp. Schooner, sailed out of Herring Neck, Captain Randolph Batstone master. Sank at Murphy's Island, Job's Cove Bight while en route to St. John's with a load of herring and fish 15 Dec 1930. Only two survived out of a crew of six.

Wasp. Schooner, Captain Coffin master. Lost at Petty Harbour en route to St. John's from PEI Nov 1850. Five men drowned.

Waterwitch. Schooner, sailed out of Brigus. Lost at Horrid Gulch near Pouch Cove, 29 Nov 1873. Eleven of the 20 on board were saved through the heroic efforts of the fishermen of Pouch Cove. Alfred Moore was awarded a medal by the Royal Humane Society for his heroism in allowing himself to be lowered over a 500 foot cliff to come to the aid of the survivors.

William Carson. Ferry, sunk off the Labrador coast 2 June 1977. No loss of life.

Wolf, SS. The second sealing steamer of that name was lost at the ice 12 Mar 1896. The original *Wolf* sank in the spring of 1871.

Bibliography

Anspach, Louis Rev., *A History of Newfoundland,* London, 1827.

Brown Cassie & Horwood H., *Death On The Ice,* Toronto, 1972.

Chappell E. T. *Voyage of H.M.S. Rosamond,* London. 1818.

Devine & O'Mara, *Noteable Events,* St. John's 1900.

Hatton & Harvey, *Newfoundland,* Boston 1883.

Innis Harold, *The Cod Fishery,* Toronto, 1954.

Mosdell H.M., *When Was That?"* St. John's 1923.

Peacock Kenneth, *Songs of the Newfoundland Outports,* Ottawa, 1965.

Prowse D. J. Judge, *The History of Newfoundland,* London 1896.

Smallwood J. R., *The Books of Newfoundland,* Vols. 1, 2, 3, 4, 5, 6, St. John's, 1937, 1967 and 1975.

Smallwood J. R., *Encyclopedia of Newfoundland,* Vols. 1 & 2, St. John's, 1981 and 1984.

Wix Ed. Rev., *Six Months of a Newfoundland Missionary's Journal,* London, 1833.

NEWSPAPERS:

The Newfoundlander, 1828, 1835, 1875.

The Public Ledger, 1867, 1875.

The Evening Telegram, 1900, 1915, 1923.

The Newfoundland Quarterly, 1914, 1976, 1977.

PAPERS & DOCUMENTS

GN 2 1/a p. Newfoundland Archives, Colonial Bldg., St. John's

C.O. 194/37, Colonial Archives.

C.O. 194/42, Colonial Archives, 511